GW00600799

Welcome

to the Complete Guide to the iPad Air

Whether you are new to the iPad or you've been using an Apple tablet since their launch in 2010, you can get more from your device. And we can show you how.

Since its launch the iPad has been called many things, but no-one ever accused it of being anything other than a truly desirable gadget. Your iPad Air will elicit 'want one' groans from friends, family and colleagues. An Apple tablet is a nice thing to own.

But despite the claims made that we are living in a 'post-PC world', the chances are your iPad won't replace your desktop or laptop PC any more than will your microwave replace your cooker. The iPad is something other than a PC – or indeed a smartphone. And while, for some people, the iPad may become an additional device to carry, for readers of *The Complete Guide to the iPad Air* it will become a critical tool and a fun toy. And a truly portable one to boot.

We start by introducing you in detail to your iPad Air, and taking you to the best apps and accessories to help you make the most of your tablet. And then we move on to the meat of *The Complete Guide to the iPad Air*: simple but detailed tutorials offering tips and tricks that help you do everything from capture and edit video, to getting the latest news, chatting with friends and managing your daily timetable.

CONTACTS

Editor in chief	Matt Egan
	matt_egan@idg.co.uk
Editor	Mark Hattersley
Editor	Rosemary Hattersley
Managing editor	Marie Brewis
Art director	Mandie Johnson

CIRCULATION & MARKETING

Marketing manager	Ash Patel

PUBLISHING

Publishing director	Simon Jary
Managing director	Kit Gould

The Complete Guide to the iPad Air is a publication of IDG Communications, the world's leading IT media, research and exposition company. With more than 300 publications in 85 countries, read by more than 100 million people each month, IDG is the world's leading publisher of computer magazines and newspapers. IDG Communications, 101 Euston Road, London NW1 2RA. This is an independent journal not affiliated with Apple Computer. Apple, the Apple logo, Mac, and Macintosh are registered trademarks of Apple Computer. All contents © IDG 2013, except when © Mac Publishing LLC.
Printer: Wyndeham Press Group Ltd - 01621 877 877
Distribution: Seymour Distribution Ltd - 020 7429 4000

32

iTunes Match

Add this computer to iCloud to share this music with your other iCloud device. You will also get access to your music in iCloud from this computer.

No Thanks   Add This Computer

112

132

contents

6 Everything iPad
Your quick-start guide to getting the iPad up and running. Discover how to use all its features in a few easy steps

Features

16 Inside the iPad Air
We take apart the iPad Air to see what's on the inside. Find out what powers Apple's tablet

18 Speed testing the iPad Air
Discover just how much faster the new iPad Air is than other iPads, and why

20 Get to know 4G LTE
There's a faster type of mobile internet in the iPad Air. Learn all about 4G internet

22 Say hello to Siri
Start using the iPad's voice-activated personal assistant. Our guide will get you talking

Buyers guide

26 Hot iPad accessories
There are some amazing gadgets and gizmos available for the iPad. Here's our pick

32 The 30 must-have apps
Add yet more functionality to your iPad with the finest apps. We find the best apps for you

Final word

160 Good enough for mum?
Jason Snell on why he thinks the iPad is the Apple device that will win over everybody

Tutorials

Everything
iPad Air

Get to know your way around one of the most amazing devices ever created

W e don't need to tell you that the iPad Air is an exceptional device. It features the first ever 64-bit processor found in a tablet, and is both smaller and lighter than the previous iPad. In the three years since Apple first unveiled the iPad, the touchscreen gadget has rightly become known as the tablet that rules all others. As well as its impressive looks, the iPad has won accolades and earned adoration the world over for its superb build and unsurpassed usability. Not for nothing was its British designer Jonathan Ive knighted by the Queen for his contribution to industrial design.

Every model has had revisions and subtle improvements that have made the world-famous tablet better than the one before. We don't know about you, but we can't wait to get started.

The iPad has won accolades and earned adoration the world over

Get to know the iPad Air

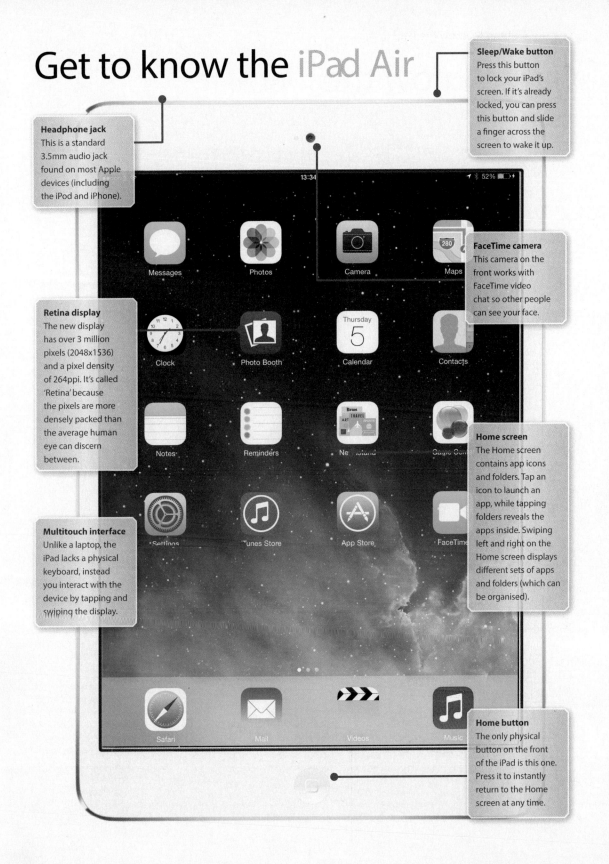

Sleep/Wake button
Press this button to lock your iPad's screen. If it's already locked, you can press this button and slide a finger across the screen to wake it up.

Headphone jack
This is a standard 3.5mm audio jack found on most Apple devices (including the iPod and iPhone).

FaceTime camera
This camera on the front works with FaceTime video chat so other people can see your face.

Retina display
The new display has over 3 million pixels (2048x1536) and a pixel density of 264ppi. It's called 'Retina' because the pixels are more densely packed than the average human eye can discern between.

Home screen
The Home screen contains app icons and folders. Tap an icon to launch an app, while tapping folders reveals the apps inside. Swiping left and right on the Home screen displays different sets of apps and folders (which can be organised).

Multitouch interface
Unlike a laptop, the iPad lacks a physical keyboard, instead you interact with the device by tapping and swiping the display.

Home button
The only physical button on the front of the iPad is this one. Press it to instantly return to the Home screen at any time.

Get to know the iPad air

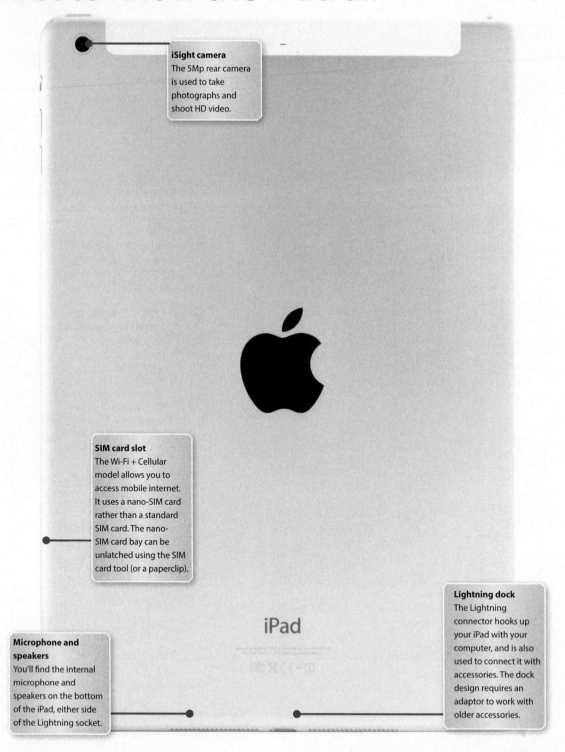

iSight camera
The 5Mp rear camera is used to take photographs and shoot HD video.

SIM card slot
The Wi-Fi + Cellular model allows you to access mobile internet. It uses a nano-SIM card rather than a standard SIM card. The nano-SIM card bay can be unlatched using the SIM card tool (or a paperclip).

Lightning dock
The Lightning connector hooks up your iPad with your computer, and is also used to connect it with accessories. The dock design requires an adaptor to work with older accessories.

Microphone and speakers
You'll find the internal microphone and speakers on the bottom of the iPad, either side of the Lightning socket.

Get to know iPad symbols

Status symbols let you know what's going on with the iPad

Like a Mac's menu bar, the top of the iPad's screen displays a number of status icons – shorthand for various settings and connections. The icons that tell you what tablet, internet or other connection your device is making are visible in the upper lefthand corner, while icons in charge of the device's other functions appear on the right. This at-a-glance guide explains what each symbol means.

Signal strength These bars indicate the current 3G, 4G and LTE strength. They fluctuate between one circle (little to no service) and five (strongest reception)

Wi-Fi strength You'll see this symbol if you're connected to a Wi-Fi network. The stronger the signal, the more bars you'll see (between one to three)

3G If you are connected to a 3G data network you will see this icon. This should enable you to use the internet and data-connected apps with ease

4G If you're lucky enough to be on a 4G network plans, and are in a 4G zone, then you'll see this icon. Your internet will be blazing-fast on 4G

LTE LTE is similar to 4G. If you are on a LTE network you should see faster internet access and be able to use data-connected apps with ease

Bluetooth Turn on Bluetooth and you'll see this icon. By default the symbol is grey, but if you connect to a Bluetooth device the symbol will turn blue

VPN This icon appears when you connect to a Virtual Private Network (VPN). Use a VPN to securely access your corporate or private network

Battery status The battery-status icon shows how much charge your iPad battery has left. A lightning bolt icon to the right of this indicates charging

Location Services When an app such as Apple Maps is using Location Services, this purple pointer will appear to the left of the iPad's battery icon

Orientation lock You can lock your iPad's display in portrait mode by double-tapping the Home button and scrolling to the left

Alarm Clock When you have an alarm set in the Clock app, this small clock appears to the right of the time at the top of your iPad

Airplane Mode Turn on Airplane Mode in Control Centre or the Settings menu to switch off all tablet, internet and Bluetooth connections. You will still be able to access your email and the web over Wi-Fi and use other iPad features

Processing icon When your iPad is trying to make a network connection, it says 'Searching…' in the upper-left corner. This circle appears if it is looking for items to sync to iCloud over your network, Wi-Fi or Bluetooth

Get to know iPad gestures

Discover how to interact with the iPad with these finger gestures

Although Apple has designed the iPad to be simple to learn, sometimes you may want a primer on the basics. Here's a breakdown of the major multitouch gestures, navigation, Home screen tips and tricks and multitasking features you'll need to master your iOS device.

Gestures and techniques

If you've never before owned a multitouch device from Apple, you may be unfamiliar with crazy phrases such as pinch-to-zoom and the difference between flick and swipe. Have no fear: while some of these gestures may have odd names, they're easy enough to pick up.

Tap: As clicking is to a desktop computer, so is tapping to an iOS device. Tapping is the most common and basic gesture.

Double-tap: Tap an object twice in succession to effect a double-tap. Double-taps are primarily used for zooming in or out on text.

Tap, hold and drag: For some functions, such as highlighting text, copying and pasting or deleting and moving apps, you'll need to tap and hold down on the screen. When you do this on a piece of text, it will highlight in blue, and editing handles – vertical lines with blue dots – will appear on either side of the highlighted area. You can tap, hold and, while holding down, drag your finger to increase or decrease the selection.

Flick and swipe: Swiping is one of your primary navigational tools: you use a left- or right swipe to move through app pages on your Home screen or images in the Photos app; you use an up or down swipe to read text in Safari, iBooks, Newsstand or elsewhere. It's one of the easiest gestures to learn.

Pinch: To zoom in or to open something, place your thumb and index finger, pinched together, onscreen and spread them apart. To zoom out, do the reverse.

Rotate: You can even rotate some elements with two or more fingers. Just place two fingers on the screen and make a circular gesture, clockwise or counterclockwise.

Get to know the Home screen

Discover how to navigate and customise your iPad's main display

Now that you've taken your first step into the iOS world with multitouch gestures, it's time to learn how to navigate your device. We'll go over where your apps are stored, how to organise, search and delete them.

The Home screen

When you first turn on your iPad Air, you're brought to the Home screen. Here, you'll see an assortment of icons grouped into rows, and several more icons grouped in the translucent Dock along the bottom of the screen. The Home screen is where your apps live, and where you can launch them.

The Dock The translucent bar along the bottom of your Home screen is called the Dock. If you've tried swiping between app pages, you'll notice the icons in the Dock don't change; the Dock is for the six apps used most frequently.

Using apps Tap an app to open it, and press the Home button to return to the Home screen.

Using and organising apps

Open and close an app To open an app, simply tap its icon. Once it's open, you can return to the Home screen at any time by pressing the Home button.

Rearrange and delete apps To rearrange the order of your icons, tap and hold any icon on the Home screen. After a few seconds, all your app icons, including the one you're holding, will start to wiggle, and a small black X will pop up in each icon's top-left corner. Once they do this, you can rearrange any apps on the Home screen, or even drag them into or out of the Dock.

If you've installed a third-party app you don't want anymore, you can tap the X to delete it (you cannot delete the apps that came preinstalled on your device). When you're finished, press the Home button, and your icons will stop wiggling and stay in their new location.

Use folders A folder is a group of apps, represented by a single icon, on your Home screen. To create a folder, start by pressing and holding your finger on any app icon to enter edit mode; after the icons begin to wiggle, drag an app on top of another app. When you release the app, you'll create a folder, which will open and display both apps. The iPad will guess at a name for the folder based on the types of apps, but you can change the name of the folder by tapping on it and editing the text with the keyboard.

The multitasking window Quickly double-press the Home button and the Multitasking bar window will appear. This displays the apps most recently run and you can slide left and right. To switch to a different app, tap its window.

Control Centre Swipe up from the bottom of the display for further controls. The Control Centre enables you to turn on and off key features, such as Wi-Fi and Bluetooth, and has Music controls.

Search in Spotlight

Swipe down on the Home screen to access Spotlight. Use the keyboard to search for apps, contacts, mail, messages, events and all other kinds of information on your iPad.

Get to know iMessages

Discover clever ways to share messages with your friends

In common with just about every tablet, the iPad is brilliant at messaging. The iPad has an exceptional app called iMessage that lets you exchange text-only SMS (Short Message Service) messages and photos and video MMS (Multimedia Messaging Service) messages with other mobile devices. When messaging another iPad or iOS user, it does far more.

Mixed messages

To start a message, tap the Messages app on the Home screen, and then tap the new message icon (a box with a pencil). You can enter a recipient's mobile number, type a contact's name or tap the Add icon (top-right) to choose an existing contact from your Contacts list. Use regular text messages when sending messages to non-Apple mobile tablets. Use the keyboard to type out your messages and press Send.

Text to talk You can send SMS-style messages to other people using Apple's iMessages service.

Making FaceTime video calls

The iSight camera on the iPad is ideal for conducting video chats

Conducting webcam-based calls on a laptop or PC is nothing new. FaceTime extends the concept of video chatting to tablets. You need a Wi-Fi or cellular network connection and for whoever you're calling to have a FaceTime-compatible device (these include iPads, iPhones, iPod touch and some Mac OS X computers).

To initiate a FaceTime call you tap on the FaceTime app icon. You'll need to enter your Apple ID and Password.

A list of names will appear from your Contacts, tap on one to start a FaceTime conversation (they will need to also be using an Apple device). They will be presented with a screen allowing him or her to decide whether to accept your FaceTime request. If they accept it, FaceTime will launch and both callers will appear onscreen.

FaceTime works over cellular as well as Wi-Fi, but you may need to turn it on by going to Settings, FaceTime and enabling the 'Use Cellular Data' setting. Be careful of how much data you use though.

Get some FaceTime Press the FaceTime button, indicated by the video camera icon, to start your video-chatting session.

Get to know notifications

Everything that's happening on your iPad in one place

Notification Centre is an exceptionally useful feature in iOS 7. Notifications are messages about things that are happening on your tablet. They can be anything from a missed call to an app update or what's in your daily calendar. Notifications often flash on the top of the screen, or appear as an alert.

However, you can access all your notifications at once using the Notification Centre. This is accessed by sliding down your finger from the top of the screen. Note that it has to be from the very top of the screen, and it's usually better to start off the top part of the iPad and work your way down.

There are three parts to Notification Centre: Today, All and Missed. Today is the default view and shows you the local weather, events in the Calendar app, items from Reminders and – if you scroll down – stocks and messages for tomorrow.

Tapping All opens Notification Centre to a wider range of messages. Here you'll see missed calls and recent messages, social media activity and updates to apps on the iPad.

Finally the Missed tab enables you to view alerts and activity that you have overlooked. These are often messages and reminders that you didn't notice first time around.

When you've finished with Notification Centre simply drag it back up and off the top of the screen.

What's going on? Notification Centre displays all the events and alerts taking place on your iPad.

Using Control centre

Quickly access all the key settings on your iPad

Control Centre is a feature-packed part of iOS 7 that can be thought of as a complement to Notification Centre.

You access Control Centre by sliding your finger up from the bottom of the screen. It's best to start all the way from the bottom of the screen and, if you're on the Lock screen, it's best to aim from the central point above the Home button.

Control Centre is absolutely packed with features. At the top are five icons that are used to turn on or off key features on the iPad: Airplane Mode, Wi-Fi, Bluetooth, Do Not Disturb and Screen Lock (this final option locks the orientation of the screen, which is useful for some apps such as iBooks). Below that is a Brightness slider, move it left to dim the screen and to the right to brighten it.

Then comes a set of controls for the Music app (and other audio). The top slider is used to control the playback position

Next are two buttons for AirDrop and AirPlay: AirDrop is used to share items such as photos and web pages with nearby people; AirPlay is used to stream music and movies to speakers and your TV.

Finally there two useful buttons at the bottom: Clock accessed the World Clock and the Camera allows you to quickly take photographs with your iPad.

Pick and choose Control Centre is jam-packed with useful buttons, sliders and options.

Get to know Siri

Apple's voice-controller is now a better listener - and much, much smarter

Siri allows you to speak commands to your tablet and have it do your bidding. In iOS 7 Siri has become much faster, and better at coming up with the feature you're looking for. It's one of the flashiest features on the iPad.

Start up Siri

You activate Siri the same way as you did Voice Control on older iPads: by holding down the Home button on the iPad itself, or by holding down the control button on your wired or wireless headset.

What to say? You can ask Siri to do all kinds of things. It's great at working with text messages – simply say: "Send a text to Dave that says 'Hello, what time are we meeting tonight?'" and Siri will do exactly that (if you know more than one Dave, it'll ask you which one – so you'll need to speak out your answer). Excitingly, you can also do the same with your emails.

What does Siri know?

It knows a lot about weather and restaurants, sports and movie times. Apple says that understanding the words you say is the easy part, and that Siri's true genius is in figuring out what you want when you say those words and getting you the answer. Siri now also works with Apple's Maps application in the UK, so you can search for directions and local businesses.

Speak and spell When you get a text message, you can instruct Siri to read the message. You can then tell Siri to reply to the message, dictate the entire message, have Siri read it back to you to confirm that it makes sense and then send it.

Wake me up It's much easier to set an alarm or timer using Siri than it is to unlock your tablet, find the Clock app and tap within the app. Just say: "Set a timer for three minutes," and your tablet begins to count down until your tea is ready. "Set an alarm for 5am" does so instantly.

Take note "Remind me to record my favourite show" and "Note that I need to take my suit to the cleaners" work, too. These are short bursts of data input that can be handled quickly by voice, and they work well.

What's special about Siri? Users not only can talk to Siri as if it were a person, they seem to want to. Beyond merely understanding what you have to say, Siri works because it has a personality. Siri's personality is one of its biggest draws. It's not just fun, but funny. When you ask Siri the meaning of life, it tells you "42" or "All Evidence to date points to chocolate."

Natural talking Talk to Siri naturally and it'll get back to you with answers quickly. You can ask Siri all kinds of things.

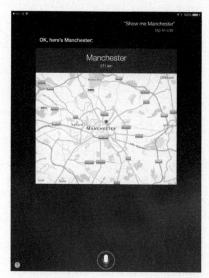

Search and go You can ask Siri for directions to places, or search for local businesses. Results from Maps appear.

Become a touchscreen typist

Tips and tricks that make using the iPad keyboard easier

For many, the biggest challenge of the iPad is getting used to the virtual keyboard. In fact, there are lots of ways Apple ensures touchscreen typing is a positive experience if you're coming from a full-size computer keyboard or a thumb-based tablet. Here are some ways to tap into the iPad's typing features.

Catch and release

The iPad registers the key you've pressed when you take your finger off the key, rather than when you tap on it. So if you press a key and see that it's the wrong one, you can easily slide your finger to the correct key. In conventional typing it's common to try and avoid pressing multiple keys; with the iPad there's no need: it recognises only single keys at once, while its correction tools work out what you meant to type.

Punctuation slide

To add a punctuation mark, press and hold the .?123 button until the numeric and punctuation keyboard appears, slide your finger to the key you want, and release. Not only will you type the punctuation mark, but you'll find yourself back in alphabet mode without having to press the ABC key.

Unlock Caps Lock

Typing in all caps may be considered impolite, but sometimes it's necessary. The Caps Lock functionality isn't enabled by default; to turn it on, go to Settings: General: Keyboard and tap on 'Enable Caps Lock'. Then, when you're typing, quickly double-tap the Shift key; it'll turn blue to tell you Caps Lock is on. Tap on it once more to disable Caps Lock.

Present and correct

No matter how good a typist you are, mistakes happen. Fortunately, the iPad's pretty smart. By looking at the letters near the ones you typed, it can deduce with surprising accuracy what you meant to type and offer the suggestion in a text bubble. To accept the suggestion, press the spacebar or a punctuation mark. To reject it, tap on the suggestion and it'll go away. Dismiss the iPad's suggestion for the same word twice, and it'll add the word you typed to its dictionary.

Zoom in

If you discover a typo, it's easy enough to fix. Tap on the spot where you want the cursor to appear, and then tap on backspace to clear your mistake. Controlling the cursor this way can be challenging. For more precise results, tap and hold on the text to make a magnifying loupe appear. As you drag the loupe around, the text-insertion point will follow it so you can position the cursor exactly where you want.

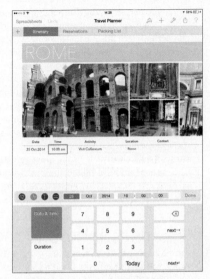

Dynamic keys The iPad keyboard changes automatically depending on what needs to be entered.

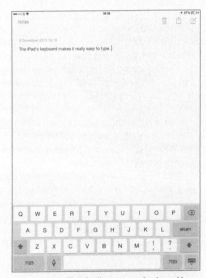

Soft machine The iPad's onscreen keyboard has large buttons that make it easy to type accurately and quickly.

Inside the iPad Air

Discover the amazing tech inside the iPad Air. By iFixit.com

When you hold a iPad in your hands for the first time, you realise just how incredible a piece of engineering it really is. The iPad comprises an ultra-powerful display with a full multitouch interface and a few slender buttons – all held within a superbly crafted (and incredibly slender) case.

As when it first launched, the iPad does feel somewhat 'magical' to use. It's not that you can't figure out how it works (it's a tablet computer, after all), but with so much contained in such a small space you find it difficult to believe how Apple has managed to cram it all in.

So what does the iPad contain? Our friends at iFixIt (ifixit.com) are experts at taking apart technical devices (and showing people how to fix them). They've taken apart the iPad Air, stripped it down and discovered what hides behind the screen and what holds it all together. Let's take a look inside.

iPad Air technical specifications

- 9.7in in-plane-switching LCD with 2048x1536 resolution at 264ppi
- Dual-core A7 CPU with 64-bit architecture
- M7 motion-tracking co-processor
- 5Mp rear iSight camera capable of recording 1080p video; 1.2Mp 720p front-facing camera
- 802.11n dual-antenna MIMO Wi-Fi
- Support for 14 LTE bands, DC-HSPA+, UMTS, GSM/EDGE, CDMA and EVDO; 16-, 32-, 64- or 128GB storage

1 Open it up

As usual, Apple has secured the digitiser glass in place with more than ample amounts of adhesive. Little screws can drive you batty but, lucky for us, we've got our Pro Tech Screwdriver Set. This LCD's connected – but not for long.

2 The battery

The Air's 3.73 V, 32.9Wh, two-cell power plant is less monstrous than the previous iPad's 43Wh, three-cell behemoth.

3 Off with its screen

The 9.7in display's specs remain unchanged from the iPad's previous outing, but Apple claims an uncanny 20 percent reduction in panel thickness. Our display, model LP097QX2, was supplied by LG.

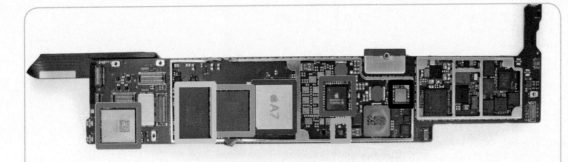

4 Getting the logic

This is the brains of the iPad Air. The logic board contains all the different chips.

- Apple APL5698 A7 Processor – a slightly different version from the APL0698 in the iPhone 5s
- Elpida F8164A1MD 1GB LPDDR3 SDRAM
- Toshiba THGBX2G7B2JLA01 16GB NAND flash
- NXP LPC18A1 (Apple M7 motion co-processor)
- Apple 343S0655-A1 – from our friends at Chipworks, this looks to be a Dialog Power Management IC
- USI 339S0213 Wi-Fi module
- Apple 338S1116 Cirrus Audio Codec, also found in the iPhone 5c

5 The big picture

iFixIt.com's Repairability score: ★☆☆☆☆

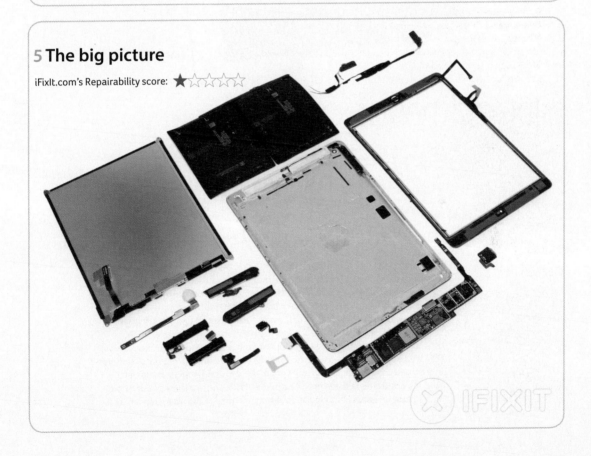

Speed testing the
iPad Air

How fast are Apple's latest iPads? We find out

Discovering just how much faster the iPad is than other Apple devices is a scientific endeavour. We have multiple speed tests on the iPad Air and iPad mini, compared to other Apple iOS devices. The results are impressive: the iPad Air is pretty much the fastest iOS device ever, while the iPad mini with Retina display is much, much faster than last year's iPad mini.

The Geekbench testing app showed the iPad Air to be faster even than the other iOS device running Apple's new A7 processor, the iPhone 5s. (The iPad Air's A7 runs a little faster than the iPhone's, owing to its larger battery and possibly its greater ability to dissipate heat.) And it was almost (but not quite) double the speed of its predecessor, the fourth-generation iPad. In essence, Apple has almost doubled the speed of the iPad.

The iPad Air also aced the two web-browsing tests we tried: the Peacekeeper HTML 5 test and the SunSpider JavaScript test. Results were similar to the Geekbench tests: in the vicinity of double the speed of the previous iPad, and slightly faster than the iPhone 5s.

Looking at the mini

Although the iPad mini with Retina display felt completely responsive and never lagged in use, our speed testing showed that it's not running at quite the same speed as the reigning iOS speed champ, the iPad Air. That's because the iPad mini's A7 processor runs at a slightly lower clock speed than the one in the iPad Air. In real-life use, though, we're not sure the speed difference between the two matters much.

The iPad Air aced the two web-browsing tests

The difference in speed between the iPad mini with Retina display and the original iPad mini, however, is dramatic. The new iPad mini is five times faster than last year's model. Geekbench scores for the Retina model were five times that of the original model; in web-based tests the Retina scores were roughly three times that of the original.

Battery life

On the battery front, Apple seems to have decided that iPads should last for about 10 hours. That's been the target since day one, and the company keeps designing its products to hit that number. That's why the Retina iPad mini's battery is so much more capacious than the original iPad mini's, and that engineering effort has paid off.

In our lab tests (which involve looping HD videos until the iPad gives up the ghost), the iPad mini with Retina lasted an impressive 10 hours, 42 minutes. That's actually longer than the iPad Air lasted – in the same test the Air ran out of juice just a couple of minutes shy of 10 hours.

iPad Air and IPad mini with Retina Display compared to other Apple devices

	Geekbench 3 Single Core	Geekbench 3 Multicore	Peacekeeper HTML 5	SunSpider 1.0.2
iPad Air	1480	2683	1844	375
Retina iPad mini	1389	2514	1770	411
iPad mini	262	493	536	1296
iPhone 5s	1416	2562	1794	405.6
iPhone 5c	709	1279	907	752
	Higher is better	Higher is better	Higher is better	Lower is better

Faster browsing with 4G LTE

Discover how to access the next generation of mobile internet

The iPad 4 is equipped with the facility to use 4G internet. At last things are looking up for UK buyers, since most of the major networks are now all offering some form of 4G connectivity.

Here's how to get 4G internet connectivity with either an iPad Air or iPad mini, and answers to (hopefully) all your questions about 4G.

What is 4G all about? It's the fourth-generation mobile internet network, which allows you to get faster, more reliable, web access on your tablet than you're used to at the moment. Several major networks in the UK are offering 4G, including EE, Vodafone, O2 and Three.

EE uses 4G Long Term Evolution (LTE) technology, which has a theoretical speed of 100Mb/s (megabits per second). EE told us: "Average 4G download speeds are likely to be between 8- and 10Mb/s, with possible instances of up to 40Mb/s. Typical upload speeds are between 5- and 6Mb/s, with possible instances of up to 15Mb/s. Typical 4G latency is only 60- to 70 milliseconds (ms), while 3G latency is typically 100- to 125ms. You can appreciate the difference if you're flicking through web pages or playing online games."

> You should expect a typical speed of between 8-12 Mbps

Who the heck is EE? It's a network formed out of Orange and T-Mobile. EE is a standalone brand that operates alongside Orange and T-Mobile – these will remain as brands and retailers in their own right. All three use the EE network; therefore smartphones and tablets will display 'EE' instead of 'Orange' or 'T-Mobile'. All existing Orange and T-Mobile stores will also be rebranded to EE and will serve customers of all three brands.

Do I need an new SIM? Probably. You'll need to get a nano-SIM for your new iPad (that's the new smaller type introduced with the iPhone 5) and most networks (apart from Three) require you to get a 4G-enabled SIM. You simply insert it into your iPad Air or iPad mini Wi-Fi + Cellular model (it goes without saying that you'll need the Wi-Fi + Cellular model). You'll need a separate nano-SIM to the one used in your phone, and you'll need to take out a separate contract for each device.

Can I get it where I live? It depends on the network you are using. The rollout from EE has seen a total of 141 towns and cities covered; whereas Three covers only London, Birmingham and Manchester so far (although

Speedier browsing 4G LTE technology enables much faster browsing and lower latency, which makes viewing web pages and streaming video more enjoyable.

more cities will receive coverage soon). Each network provides a coverage checker that will let you know what service you can expect in your area.

How much does it cost? In the past year 4G was considerably more expensive than 3G data, but prices seem to have fallen and iPad owners looking to use 4G shouldn't have to pay more than a 3G contract owners. Here are the current pay-as-you-go prices for each network:

EE (1GB) – £10 (30 days)
O2 (1GB) – £10 (30 days)
Vodafone - £10 (30 days)
Three - £7.50 (per month)

What happens if I break the limit? EE has announced that if you go over your data plan you stop getting Cellular data. It does not intend to charge you for exceeding the data plan (which is a good thing because the extra charges tend to be rather high). Check with your provider, but most offer the same sort of deal.

Which plan should I get? Your milage will vary depending on how much you use your iPad and what type of content you download. Bear in mind that 4G internet is fast, which means you're using more data more quickly. We find that 1GB is generally enough for one month's general web browsing and email. But start adding iTunes Match and streaming services such as BBC iPlayer, Netflix or LoveFilm and you may need 3- or 5GB.

Say hello to
Siri

Although the latest iPad sports a faster processor and a bold new design, the feature that everyone is still talking about is Siri. Siri enables you to speak commands to your phone and have it do your bidding. You activate Siri by holding down the Home button on the iPad itself, or by holding down the control button on your earphones. Siri is faster and more reliable than ever with iOS 7.

The iPad's voice-recognition feature works by recording your voice and sending it to a server that interprets what you've said and returns plain text. If you don't have an internet connection, Siri won't work.

Siri is a massive leap forward over old-fashioned speech recognition. This used to require a strict vocabulary and couldn't do very much. Worse still, for non-Americans, voice recognition struggled with European, Australian and other accents.

Siri doesn't require a strict vocabulary, and it'll generally figure out what you're trying to say. That makes interacting with it seem much more natural. It also works pretty well with a range of accents, and has American, British and Australian settings, as well as French, German, Italian, Spanish and more.

> Siri doesn't require a strict vocabulary, and it'll generally figure out what you're trying to say

Siri is comprehensive. It's tied into Messages, Calendar, Music, Reminders, Maps, Mail, Weather, Stocks, Clock, Contacts, Notes and Safari. It's also linked to Wolfram Alpha, the 'computational knowledge engine' that can provide answers to numerous factual questions, and Yelp, the directory of local businesses.

The recent iOS 7 update to Siri also sees it capable of searching Twitter and adjusting Settings. Siri can also perform a web search for you – although it now uses Bing as the default search engine, asking Siri to "Google" something results in it using Google instead.

Speaking your language

GETTING STARTED WITH SIRI COULDN'T BE EASIER. Simply press and hold the Home button. The background will blur, you'll hear a 'ba-ding' noise and 'What can I help you with?' appears onscreen. You should also see a wavy white line at the bottom of the screen.

Simply speak your request into the iPad and, when you've finished speaking, the white line turns into a round microphone icon and Siri will get back to you with an answer. Sometimes it takes Siri a few moments to think about the answer, but it's a lot faster in iOS 7.

You can ask Siri all sorts of things, and the more you use Siri the more accurate it becomes. You soon become aware of just how useful it can be, and what its boundaries are. It knows a lot about weather, restaurants, movies and football, for example, but nothing about Formula One.

It is also hooked-up to the Maps application, so it can locate businesses, movie times, restaurants and bars near you. One of the great things about Siri is asking it to find things in your local area.

There are a few scenarios in which Siri truly excels. The first of those is when you're in a hands-free scenario, mostly likely when driving a car. (The iPad knows when you're in a hands-free situation and becomes more chatty, reading text aloud that it might not if it knows you're holding it in your hand.) Siri is also deeply integrated with the directions feature in Maps, and the iPad works as a fantastic (if slightly large) voice-activated satnav.

The more you use Siri the more accurate it becomes

When you get a message, you can instruct Siri to read the message, and it will. You can then tell it to reply to the message, dictate the entire message, have Siri read it back to you to confirm that it makes sense, and then send it. You can also ask Siri to read out your Mail messages and it'll let you know who sent you a message and what the subject line is.

There are still some gaps. Siri won't read your emails to you and it'd be great if you could get it to read out whole books and web pages. And while iOS has the nifty Notification Centre, which gives you granular control over how different apps notify you about what's going on, there's no option to read alerts out loud when you're in hands-free mode. A missed opportunity.

Talking clocks

IF YOU AREN'T DRIVING, SIRI CAN STILL BE USEFUL. In fact, the feature proves that some tasks can be done much faster through speech than through clicking, tapping and swiping. It's much easier to set an alarm

Getting better Siri can now access the iOS 7 Settings, which makes it much easier to quickly make changes. You can also ask it to search Twitter.

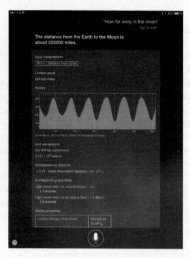

Getting results Siri can hunt down business, movie and sport information, as well as answer general questions.

or timer using Siri than it is to unlock your tablet, find the Clock app, and tap within the app. Just say, "Set a timer for three minutes," and your iPad begins to count down until your tea is ready. "Set an alarm for 5am" does what you'd expect, instantly. "Remind me to record my favourite show" and "Note that I need to take my suit to the cleaners" work, too. These are short bursts of data input that can be handled quickly by voice, and we've found they work well.

It's also much faster to ask Siri to access settings than it is to dive through the menu. You can just say "Change wallpaper" rather than opening Settings and tapping Wallpaper.

You will soon become impressed by Siri's ability to understand the context of conversations. It doesn't always work, but when it does, it's magical. We asked Siri for suggestions for places to have lunch and it provided us with a list of nearby restaurants that serve lunch.

Talking to your iPad is not much different from talking on your mobile phone. It's not appropriate in all contexts. If, for example, you're quietly reading in the library and need to set a reminder, you should use the Reminders app, not Siri. And if you're out in public, well, you can use Siri, but you do risk people giving you funny looks.

Apple's integration of Wolfram Alpha with Siri is a smart move. If you need answers to factual questions, such as the speed of light or the number of days until Christmas, the answer engine can provide the solution.

> It doesn't always work. But when it does, it's utterly magical

Personal dictation

WHILE SIRI GETS THE BULK OF THE iPAD FEATURE HYPE, another speech-related technology may prove to be more important and a bigger boost to user productivity. On the keyboard you'll see a new button in the bottom row, to the left of the spacebar, with the image of a microphone on it. Tap this button and the iPad will transcribe whatever you say. It sends the results over the internet to a server that analyses your speech and converts it into text. We were impressed at just how fast the results came back, especially over Wi-Fi. And they were generally an accurate representation of what we had said.

To get the most out of dictation, you'll need to start thinking in punctuation. For example, to construct a decent email message, we might say, "Dan. Comma. New paragraph. What do you think about writing a review of iOS numeral five. Question mark. New paragraph. Let me know what you think. Exclamation point." However, it works.

Part of Siri's charm isn't in its feature set (which is still hit and miss), but it's personable nature. Siri feels a lot less robotic than other voice-activated technology. Even when Siri gets out of its depth and doesn't know what to do, it's difficult to

Siri is one of the most entertaining aspects of the iPad… try it out

feel too frustrated. And you can joke around with Siri. Apple has spent a lot of time providing Siri with a range of comebacks to joke questions (many geeky by nature). Try telling Siri you love it, or use common catchphrases such as "Who's your daddy" or "Who let the dogs out?" These are constantly being updated, too – for example, a recent one is to keep saying "Okay Glass" (the phrase used to activate a rival product made by Google), and Siri starts to get annoyed.

Siri is by no means perfect, and occasionally it can mistranslate what you're saying, either transcribing the wrong message or finding the wrong result from Contacts. But it gets better the more you use it, and the more useful it becomes. And it's fun! Siri is one of the most entertaining aspects of the iPad, so be sure to hold down the Home button and try it out.

Wake me up One of the most useful ways to use Siri is to ask it to set alarms, timers and reminders.

Joking around Siri has a quirky sense of humour and will respond to geeky comments, flirtation and famous sayings.

The best iPad Air accessories

The iPad is fantastic by itself, but there are plenty of accessories
that you can use that make it even better

If you've been using an iPad for a while, you're likely well aware of its wide variety of accessories. But if your new iPad is your first, you may be wondering about the best accessories and add-ons.

The good news is that the market is already packed with compatible accessories. The bad news is that, for the same reason, there are so many options that you may not know where to start. Here's a quick list of the most-useful iPad accessories out there on the market.

Some of these are more essential than others. A good case is a must, as it keeps your iPad safe from scrapes and drops. Bear in mind that the iPad Air is a different size to older iPad models, which means that many iPad cases will not fit. So, when buying such a case, you should make sure that the manufacturer claims it does fit the iPad Air before parting with your cash.

Cases aside, there's a wealth of speakers, earphones, TV tuners, camera connectors and keyboards. All manner of items, in fact. So let's take a look at some of the most interesting kit on the market.

Ultrathin Keyboard

Company: **Logitech**
URL: www.logitech.com
Price: £89

The iPad Air keyboard is great to type on, but sometimes you want a physical keyboard to tap out a little faster. You can add an Apple Keyboard, but it's bulky. Logitech makes a great range of keyboards that double as iPad Air covers. This is one of our favourites, the Ultrathin Keyboard. It forms a magnetic case or flips around to create a full keyboard that's easy to type on.

Studio Neat Cosmonaut

Company: **Studio Neat**
URL: studioneat.com
Price: £15

If you're looking to paint and draw on your iPad (with apps such as Brushes) then you might want to invest in a stylus. The Cosmonaut, from US-based Studio Neat, was born out of the desire to create a great stylus that didn't try to replicate the feel of pen on paper. The makers say the idea was to feel more like a dry-erase marker, which should mean more responsive mark-making on the iPad. Despite concerns about its size and shape, with the Cosmonaut resembling a large crayon, we are impressed. The Cosmonaut offers control and precision lacking from slighter, more traditional pen-like options, working well with not only the iPad, but iPhone and iPod touchscreens, too.

Nike+ Fuelband

Company: **Nike**
URL: nikeplus.nike.com
Price: £129

Billed as the 'smarter way to keep fit', the Fuelband measures everything from your daily walking to exercise workouts. The band then hooks up with an app on your iPad to keep track of how you're doing, offer tips and encouragement, and even set challenges for you. It's a good way to stay in shape.

Withings WiFi Smart Body Analyzer and Digital Scale

Company: **Withings**
URL: withings.com
Price: £129

Keep track of your body weight, heart rate and air quality with this high-tech set of scales. It hooks up to your iPad to keep track of measurements over time, and can help you set and stick to weight goals.

Play:3 & Bridge

Company: **Sonos**
URL: sonos.com
Price: £250 (Play:3) & £42 (Bridge)

Looking for the best set of wireless speakers to go with your new iPad? Get a Sonos Play:3. With a Play:3 and a Bridge device you can bounce audio from your iPad, or Mac/PC straight to the speaker. If that wasn't good enough, the Sonos Player app brings together the audio from your Mac, iPhone, iPad, services such as Spotify and Napster, and digital radio. A truly superb speaker system.

Hover Bar

Company: **TwelveSouth**
URL: twelvesouth.com
Price: £50 (plus £15 P&P)

Every now and then a product comes along that's so crazy, yet so stunningly simple, that it becomes an instant classic. The HoverBar from TwelveSouth is one such device. It's a malleable metal arm with a clamp at one end and an iPad mount at the other, but it's how it's put to work that impresses. Attaching the clamp to any surface or object allows you to hover your device at any angle or height you require. Floating next to an iMac is an obvious solution, but the HoverBar works equally well from a bedside table, kitchen counter, car seat or anything offering an inch of available area to grip.

Wacom Creative Stylus

Company: **Wacom**
URL: wacom.com
Price: £84

The Wacom Creative Stylus gives you the tip sensitivity of a Cintiq pen – that's 2,048 levels of pressure sensitivity, fact fans – and the professional, lightweight feel shared by the other Wacom stylus products (the cheapest of which is £749). It's an amazing tool for digital artists.

Belkin WeMo

Company: **Belkin**
URL: belkin.co.uk/uk
Price: £79

WeMo is billed as a family of devices from Belkin that allows users to control home electronics via a free iOS app. You can turn on and off lights, TVs, appliances and more via your iPad. It's a big plus if your mobility or health isn't what it could be.

Logitech UE 6000

Company: **Logitech**
URL: logitech.com
Price: £169

Logitech Ultimate Ears (UE) 6000 are a stylish set of DJ headphones that provide excellent bass, superb treble and active noise cancellation in a stylish package. If you like bass you'll be in heaven – the Logitech delivers in abundance. A stylish and powerful set of earphones.

EyeTV W

Company: **Elgato**
URL: elgato.com
Price: £69

This interesting device enables you to wirelessly stream digital Freeview television to an iPhone or iPad. We think the EyeTV is a terrific system for watching live television on the iPhone and iPad. It's an ingenious solution that works quickly with a minimum amount of fuss.

Philips Hue

Company: **Phillips**
URL: philips.co.uk
Price: **£49**
This intelligent lightbulb can be controlled from your iPad, able to create different colours in various shades. Very cool.

HP Photosmart 5510

Company: **HP**
URL: hp.com/uk
Price: **£99**
The HP Photosmart 5510 is a printer you can use with your iPad (or other iOS device), thanks to Apple's AirPrint technology. This is built into the iPad and means all you have to do is connect the printer to the same wireless network, select a document, photo or Mail message and hit Print. It's difficult to find fault with HP's Photosmart Premium: it's fast, versatile and produces very good-quality prints, and it has a great price to boot.

Lightning to 30-pin Adaptor

Company: **Apple**
URL: apple.com/uk
Price: **£30**
Lightning replaced the 30-pin connection that has been used on most Apple devices since the introduction of the original iPod. With such a legacy behind it the change is something of a shock to many long-term Apple fans, who now find themselves having to deal with a device that doesn't physically fit many of the accessories they own.

Fortunately, Apple has released this Lightning to 30-pin Adaptor that enables you to attach older 30-pin dock devices and cables to the latest iPad.

Using the adaptor is easy enough. Plug one end into the iPad and the other into the accessory.

It enables you to charge and sync most devices. The only thing it doesn't do is support video output, for which you'll need the Digital Adaptor.

Pioneer A3

Company: **Pioneer**
URL: pioneer.eu/uk
Price: **£269**
The iPad can stream audio directly to some speakers using AirPlay. These speakers aren't cheap, but they support AirPlay and feature great audio quality and a built-in battery so you can use them outside. They're a great buy for anybody looking to use the iPad as a music system.

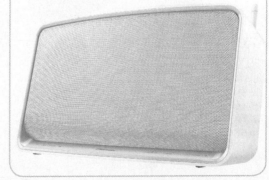

Apple TV

Company: **Apple**
URL: apple.com/uk
Price: **£99**

The Apple TV is one of Apple's lesser-known products, but don't underestimate the power of Apple's diminutive TV device: it's a fantastic piece of kit to have in the home. The Apple TV enables you to buy, download and stream content from iTunes on your television (you can rent and download movies); it has support for Netflix; and you can stream and play music, podcasts, videos and photos from a Mac or PC, or directly from your iPad. While it still lacks some functionality that we'd like (there's no BBC iPlayer support, for example), it's the easiest way to stream iTunes content to your TV.

Celestron NexStar

Company: **Celestron**
URL: celestron.com
Price: **£499**

This computerised telescope enables you to view the stars right from your iPad. The Skyalign system can find stars, planets and nebulae simply by calling them up using the SkyQ app. The 5in aperture provides spectacular views.

Smart Key

Company: **Elgato**
URL: elgato.com
Price: **£33**

This Smart Key is an innovative Bluetooth dongle that you attach to your keys. It then communicates with your iPad, which will alert you if you leave your keys behind (or can play a sound if you've lost them). You can also put the Smart Key in your bag or suitcase, and your iPad will alert you if you leave it behind. Or you can place one in your car, and you'll never lose your place in the car park.

It's a quirky accessory, but one that promises to be massively useful.

Smart Cover

Company: **Apple**
URL: apple.com/uk
Price: £35

The Smart Cover clips on to the side of the new iPad using two magnets and a clever clamp that makes it easy to attach and remove, while simultaneously ensuring that it doesn't slip off. Another set of magnets clamp it to the screen of the new iPad, and opening and closing the Smart Cover wakes up and puts to sleep the device.

The Smart Cover can also fold into a triangle to form a stand for the iPad for more comfortable typing, while its interior micro-fibre surface helps to keep the screen clean.

What the Smart Cover doesn't do particularly well is protect the iPad, which is a virtually solid piece of glass that will happily shatter if you drop it on to concrete.

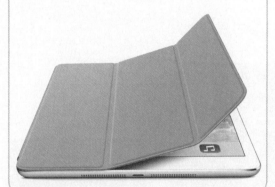

Digital AV Adapter

Company: **Apple**
URL: apple.com/uk
Price: £39

This handy little adaptor enables you to mirror anything you see on your iPad's screen on a HDTV. It's useful if you want a quick and easy way to show off what's on your iPad without investing in an Apple TV.

While it's not as versatile as an Apple TV it's also a third of the price, and can be carried around with you. The Digital AV Adaptor is a great way to play video, stream audio, and show off photos. It's also useful for doing presentations.

A second Dock connector input enables you to keep your iPad on charge while streaming the video out to the HDTV, which is great when playing long movies.

IK Multimedia iRig KEYS

Company: **IK Multimedia**
URL: ikmultimedia.com
Price: £109

This MIDI keyboard features 37 velocity-sensitive keys and a MIDI interface to connect to the iPad. It's perfect for musicians looking to make, record and edit audio using the iPad.

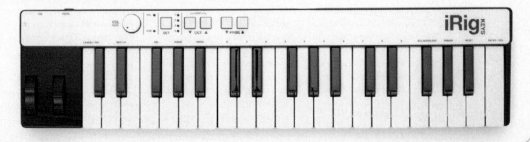

The
30 best apps

Our picks from the App Store gems

The headline feature of the iPad is its fast A7 processor and Retina screen. And what a thing of beauty is the latter. Crisp, vibrant and sharper than a vintage *Monty Python* sketch, it truly needs to be seen to be believed. Tech this good deserves to be taken advantage of. So, to help you put your new tablet through its paces, we've compiled a list of the best A7-ready apps on the App Store.

Minecraft
Price: £4.99

If you haven't yet discovered the pleasures of Minecraft, be very careful. This is a game that can easily vacuum up huge swathes of your life. And it all comes from such a simple concept, too. You build in this world by collecting blocks. First, you collect wood from trees. Later, when you've made the tools to do so, you can dig into the earth or carve caves out of rock. Minecraft has a vast inventory of materials to mine or gather, and tools you can create. It's like having a giant Lego set.

iPhoto
Price: £2.99

The iOS version of Apple's brilliantly accessible photo-editing suite is a great tool for showing off the iPad's screen. Not only does it offer unparalleled clarity when displaying your high-definition photos, but it also makes it that much easier to accurately edit your images. Unwanted blemishes are easier to spot, subtle tweaks are easier to appreciate and crops are easier to judge. Honestly, you'll want to glue a picture hook to the back of your tablet and hang it on the wall.

Infinity Blade 3
Price: £4.99

The Infinity Blade series has long been the graphical litmus test for any new iPad. And the latest edition doesn't disappoint. Infinity Blade III has already been optimised for the iPad's 64-bit processor with full-screen anti-aliasing, bloom, full-screen vignettes, distortion, high-resolution shadows, and environmental reflections. In the words of the developer, "It looks crazy awesome!" If you want to see what the new iPad is capable of, this is the game to get.

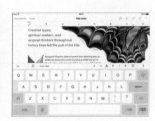

Sketchbook Pro
Price: £2.99

Not only has developer Autodesk updated its digital sketchbook app to support the iPad's Retina screen, it has also leveraged the device's increased processing power to add functionality. Artists can now make use of more layers on their images – 18 (up from 12) for the 1024x768 canvas, and six (up from four) for the 2048x1536 canvas. In short, one of the best art packages available on the system just got better, and at no extra charge. Highly recommended.

iMovie
Price: £2.99

It should come as no surprise that one of Apple's own flagship apps was among the first programs to receive an update adding support for the manufacturer's new generation of tablet tech. Full-HD footage captured with the iPad's camera looks ace at 1080p. What's more, Apple has even added extra features: new cross-app content sharing with GarageBand, a few new editing tools and the ability to cut together a Hollywood-style trailer for your movie.

Pages
Price: £6.99

Apple's word-processing app was another obvious candidate for a Retina update, and the platform holder has failed to disappoint. As well as full support for the new screen, the latest update has brought a couple of additional features. You can now include a variety of charts in your documents, and there's improved Cloud support. And on top of that, the new built-in dictation tool in the iPad's virtual keyboard really comes into its own here.

Mass Effect Infiltrator
Price: £4.99

The iOS companion piece to mega-selling PC- and console RPG Mass Effect is one the first new apps to come with Retina support as standard. The game itself is a stripped-down, arcadey take on its more nuanced and complex source material, but it's a fun 3D shooter nonetheless, and a brilliant showcase for the system's power. In a similar vein, the Dead Space app, from the same publisher and developer, also has Retina support.

Solar Walk
Price: £1.99

The fascinating interactive galactic map app was always going to benefit from the iPad's extra power, and developer Vito Technology hasn't let us down. The app now includes new high-resolution textures, slick visual effects and a handsome user interface that makes exploring our galaxy even more of a sensory assault. New space objects have been added, too, including the asteroid belt and the moons of Neptune.

Numbers
Price: £6.99

Apple hasn't wasted any time updating its Numbers spreadsheet app to take advantage of its newly empowered tablet. As well as support for that razor-sharp Retina screen, it's shoehorned in a number of performance improvements and the ability to display your data in an impressive array of 3D charts. It remains the best app of its kind on the App Store and a hugely useful office tool no matter the scope of number-crunching.

Photoshop Express is a great way of showing off the new Retina display

Real Racing 3
Price: Free

Firemint's third instalment of its best-selling racing sim has made impressive use of Apple's latest hardware update. Naturally, the already eye-popping visuals have received an additional boost thanks to the faster A7 processor. You get to race on a 22-car grid and can challenge your friends online. This is a realistic racing game that sees you driving fully licensed cars around real tracks. It's a fantastic showcase of the new iPad Air and iPad mini's power. A visual tour de force.

Labyrinth 2 HD
Price: £5.49

Labyrinth 2's core concept is as old as the hills – you tilt the playing surface to guide a marble through a maze dotted with obstacles and pitfalls. However, developer Illusion Labs has breathed new life into it on the iPad by upping the challenge and broadening the scope. It's added multiplayer, incorporated a vast array of off-the-wall elements, and included a full-featured level editor that lets you create your own stages. It also looks fantastic, thanks to a new Retina update.

Photoshop Express
Price: Free

Adobe's alternative to iPhoto isn't as slick and accessible as Apple's editing suite, but it's a solid package nonetheless, offering a range of tools, filters and special effects with which to touch up your snaps. Be warned, some of the features on offer are available only via an in-app purchase, so go in with your eyes open. As is the case with Apple's iPhoto, the newly Retina-friendly app is a great way of showing off both the iPad's amazingly detailed screen and all your images.

Keynote
Price: £6.99

Another part of Apple's office suite, Keynote lets you easily create presentations and slideshows from your iPad. Like all Apple software, it's extremely user-friendly and has a range of clever tricks to help set your work apart. You can add your own animations, incorporate media you've created in iMovie or GarageBand, and build dynamic charts and graphs, all with a few swipes of the display.

iStopMotion
Price: £6.99

iStopMotion does what it says on the tin. It's a rather brilliant package that lets you create your own stop-motion animation on your iPad. Once you've set up your scene, you can trigger a time-lapse photo sequence, which takes an image every few seconds, giving you time to move around objects and create a complete movie. It's well put together, easy to use, and adds Retina support.

Order and Chaos
Price: £4.99

Let's not beat around the bush – Order and Chaos is a fairly shameless iOS riff on the hugely popular fantasy MMO World of Warcraft. Although it wins few points for originality, Gameloft's effort scores with its moreish gameplay, classy feature set and accomplished visuals. Take note: it's a subscription title, so you have to pay a monthly fee on top of the purchase price to keep playing.

Star Walk
Price: £1.99

From the same developer behind the excellent Solar Walk app, Star Walk is an essential iOS purchase for amateur astronomers. The app offers an astonishingly detailed map of the night sky, complete with profile pages for all the main heavenly bodies. What's more, thanks to GPS, it also works in real time. Just hold up your device to the night sky and the app will overlay information about the stars visible in your display.

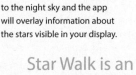

Star Walk is an essential purchase

Incredibooth
Price: 69p

Just the thing for a wild night on the town, Incredibooth lets you snap strips of photobooth-style images with friends, offering you a range of wacky filters and backdrops to up the fun factor. The results are often hilarious. It's a straightforward point-and-shoot app, but it's also very thoughtfully put together with a wide range of editing and sharing options.

Flight Control Rocket
Price: 69p

Flight Control remains one of the true App Store classics – fun, easy to pick up and impossible to put down. A few years on from its original effort, developer Firemint has unleashed a sequel of sorts, and it's every bit as addictive. The principle remains the same – you need to guide your vessels on to a series of landing pads while avoiding other air traffic. This time, the action has shifted to outer space, bringing with it a range of new gameplay possibilities. As one of the first games released in the wake of the new iPad, it fully supports the Retina display.

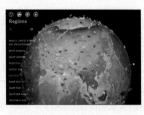

GarageBand

Price: Free

Ever fancied yourself as the next Phil Spector or Brian Eno? Well, GarageBand is the app for you. Either plug in one of your own instruments or use the virtual keyboards, drumkits and guitars included, and record your own mini-masterpiece. It's as complex and sophisticated as you want it to be: no musical ability is required. The app is free, but you have to pay for some musical instruments and sounds.

Barefoot World Atlas

Price: £5.49

This fantastic kids app is an iPad-only interactive atlas that colourfully immerses youngsters in the myriad wonders of planet Earth. It's a great way of engaging children in geography, detailing different wildlife, the world's great cities, geological features and weather systems. There's spoken narration as well as written text, vibrant photography, lovely illustrations and a massive library of sound effects and music.

iBooks

Price: Free

One of the iPad's few weaknesses is that, as an e-reader, it can't hope to match up to a Kindle's E Ink display. The tablet's more traditional screen is more difficult to read for longer periods than the competition's virtual paper. However, thanks to the iPad's Retina display, that's much less of an issue. The added clarity makes it much easier on the eye with a number of new functionality enhancements, too. Give it a try.

Need for Speed: Most Wanted

Price: £2.99

The iPad's a great device for racing games, and we've got a few in this feature. While Real Racing 3 has the realism, and Asphalt has all the action, it's this game, Need For Speed: Most Wanted, that has the graphics. One of the most visually arresting games you can buy, and it's fun, too: tearing along streets avoiding the cops!

> One of the most visually arresting games you can buy

Another Monster at the End of This Book

Price: £2.49

This 'Sesame Street' interactive story book is one of the most charming kids' apps available on the App Store. And there's a fair few young-at-heart adults who'll get some chuckles out of it, too. It's not terribly complicated – it's just a well-told story dotted with a few lively mini-games and animations designed to build youngsters' vocabulary and spatial-relations skills. And a new Retina update helps bring things to life, with vibrant colours and smooth transitions.

Touchgrind BMX

Price: £2.99

A great example of a game that could only ever work on a touchscreen device. This ingenious creation sees you pulling off BMX stunts by manipulating your bike in real time using the multitouch display. It's an ambitious concept but works beautifully in practice, offering some of the purest fun of any App Store game. In a nice touch, it even lets you record your most outrageous tricks for posterity and share them with friends. The iPad's Retina display has it looking even better than ever to boot.

Modern Combat 4
Price: £4.99

The closest thing you'll get to a full Call of Duty game on the App Store. The first-person-shooter genre isn't naturally a great fit for touchscreen controls, but Modern Combat 4 does its best within the limitations, offering a fun, slick and perfectly playable action game. It wins no points for originality – this is an app that knows exactly who is its audience – but, as shooting galleries go, this is a solid, Retina-enabled choice with great multiplayer support.

Asphalt 8: Airborne
Price: Free

This slick racer from iOS specialist Gameloft runs pretty close for pole position as the best motorsport game on the App Store. Racing is one area where the iPad utterly excels. Gameloft's Asphalt series has always led the pack, and it's new Asphalt 8 Airborne game certainly doesn't disappoint. The graphics are spectacular, with frenetic onscreen action. This is one game that you really shouldn't miss if you want to show off your iPhone and have some fun.

Evernote
Price: Free

Simply put, Evernote is one of the very best productivity apps available for iOS devices. This hugely popular piece of software lets you draw up lists, jot down reminder notes, take photos and record voice memos, and then file them by date and/or location. You can sync everything across multiple devices, email items to friends and colleagues, and post content to various social networks. It's a great way to stay organised and reduce your paper trail.

Asphalt 6's Retina-friendly visuals are up there with the best

Macworld Express
Price: Free

The Macworld Express app comes to you from the publishers of *The Complete Guide to the iPad Air* and is a great way of staying abreast of all the latest Apple news. Not only does it offer timely reporting on all the latest Apple happenings, but you also get product reviews, features and handy tutorials to help you get the best from your device. It's also fully customisable, so you'll read only the content you want. What's more, it's free to download. Do you need any other reason to give it a go? We didn't think so.

LogMeIn
Price: Free (Basic);
from £8.99 per month (Pro)

LogMeIn is an iOS app that allows users to access and remotely control work and home computers via iPad, iPhone or iPod touch, anywhere they have an active internet connection. Aimed primarily at business users, it also has much wider appeal. Setup is simple and requires users to pair the free iOS app with any computer, although that computer needs to be switched on, or at least woken from sleep to be seen. The free version is good enough for most people.

Art Authority
Price: £2.99

Art Authority is another app that shines by virtue of being on the iPad's Retina display. It's in essence the world's best art gallery distilled into your iPad. There are thousands of masterpieces available for viewing from the greatest artists the world has ever seen, including Botticelli, Leonardo da Vinci and Edvard Munch, all searchable by name or movement. On top of that, there's expert commentary, interactive timelines and a neat feature that searches for similar works in a gallery near you. A must for art lovers.

Macworld

Subscribe to

SAVE UP TO 60% ON YOUR SUBSCRIPTION

idg.subscribeonline.co.uk/subscriptions/macworld

Setting up your iPad Air for the first time

Get your iPad Air up and running without a PC or Mac

YOU'VE FINALLY GOT YOUR HANDS ON THE BRAND -new iPad Air and now it's time to get it set up and ready for use. The excitement of buying a iPad has, over the years, been tempered by the fact that to get your device up and running you were first required to plug your tablet into a computer. Whether you stood in line for two weeks to get your hands on one, or preordered for it to be delivered to your house, the rush of delight was often held in check by the necessity to wait until iTunes told you that your shiny new tablet was ready.

The iPad Air no longer needs to be physically connected to a computer first in order for it to work. As you might expect from Apple, the process is simple and quick; about the most technically difficult part is inserting the nano SIM card into the iPad Air (you need this only if you have an iPad Air Wi-Fi + Cellular model). In typical Apple style there's even a SIM-card Replacement Tool included in the box to make this task even easier.

We'll assume that you have all the boring stuff such as your tablet price plan sorted out and have unboxed and inserted the SIM card into your new iPad. From here on in it's no more than a five-minute process. Wire-free setup is a breeze and all you have to do is follow the simple steps here to make sure that you and your tablet are ready to go as quickly as possible.

After that, there's a whole world of calling, texting, tweeting, internet browsing and taking photos, as well as all the apps to enjoy.

KIT LIST:
- iPad
- SIM card
- Wi-Fi connection

Time required: 5 mins
Difficulty: Beginner

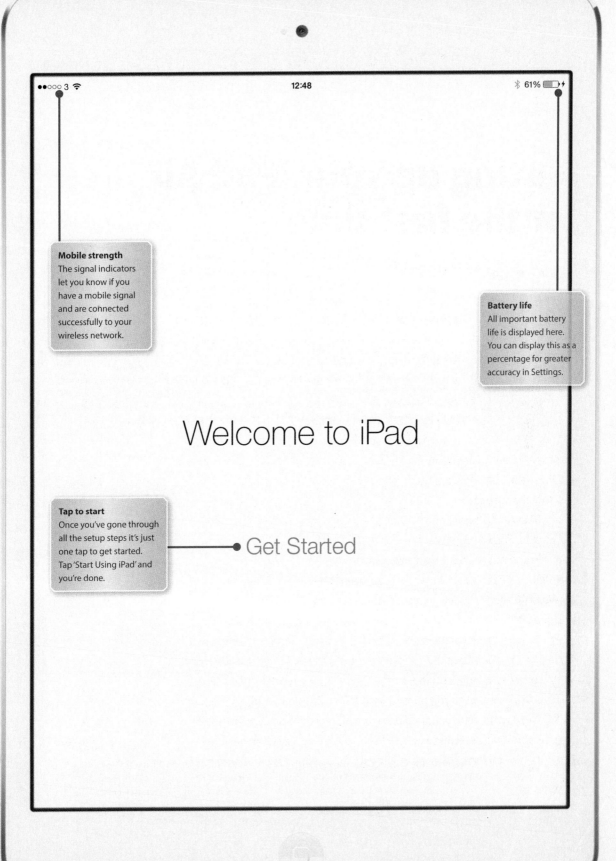

Mobile strength
The signal indicators let you know if you have a mobile signal and are connected successfully to your wireless network.

Battery life
All important battery life is displayed here. You can display this as a percentage for greater accuracy in Settings.

Welcome to iPad

Tap to start
Once you've gone through all the setup steps it's just one tap to get started. Tap 'Start Using iPad' and you're done.

Get Started

STEP-BY-STEP GUIDE: Set up your iPad Air for the first time

1 Turn on Press and hold the button on the top of the new iPad until you see the Apple logo on screen. After a few moments you'll see the above screen. Slide to your finger to the right to start.

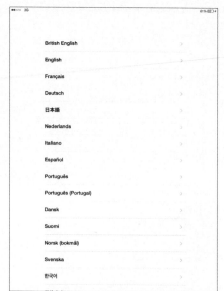

2 Pick your language The first screen lets you choose what language to use on your iPad. Tap on the language you want, then move on to the next step.

3 Where am I? Select your country next. It's likely that the new iPad will have your location as the top choice. If it's not, tap on 'Show More…' Pick your location and then tap Next.

4 Connect to Wi-Fi If you have a wireless network at home or at work you can connect to it here. Tap on the wireless network name. Alternatively, choose 'Use Mobile Connection'.

5 Location tracking If you want your new iPad and apps to know where you are – handy for mapping and social-media tools, enable this by taping 'Enable Location Services' and then Next.

6 Activation If this is your first iPad, choose 'Set Up as New iPad' and click next. Otherwise you can use iCloud or iTunes to transfer the data from one iPad to another.

Which services

After the terms and conditions you'll be asked which services (such as Location Services, Siri and iCloud) you want to use. Apple needs your permission for each service, but they're all worth using.

7 Sign in You need an Apple ID to make full use of your iPad. Click Sign In if you already have one, or 'Create a Free Apple ID' to go through the process of signing up with Apple. You're now good to go.

8 Terms and conditions Take time to read the terms and conditions. Click the blue Agree button to continue. You'll need to agree to each service (Siri, iCloud and so on) you want to use.

Wirelessly synching your iPad Air to iTunes

Cut the cord between your iPad Air and computer

SYNCHING AN iPAD AND iTUNES USED TO MEAN that you had to plug your tablet into your Mac or PC and either sit and watch the progress bar or leave it and pop back whenever you thought it might be ready. Happily, there is now a better solution to synching your iPad Air.

Now you can keep your iPad Air and iTunes account on your PC or Mac in tune without wires. No more hunting around for that white cable. Never again will you have to scrabble around under your desk as you attempt to plug the USB cable into your PC.

Wireless synching works when both your iPad Air and computer are connected to the same wireless network and your tablet is connected to a power source. You'll have to keep your computer on and running iTunes, too. This means that you can leave your iPad Air charging overnight and wake up to a fully synched tablet and iTunes.

The more content you've purchased the longer this will take, but wireless sync covers everything: applications, music, bookmarks, books, contacts calendars, movies, photos, notes, documents and ringtones are all synched wirelessly over your network.

When your iPad Air is connected to a power source and the Wi-Fi network it will show up just as it would were it plugged into your computer via a USB cable. This means you can change settings and other options wirelessly, too.

KIT LIST:
- IPad
- Wireless network
- PC or Mac with iTunes

Time required: 10 mins
Difficulty: Easy

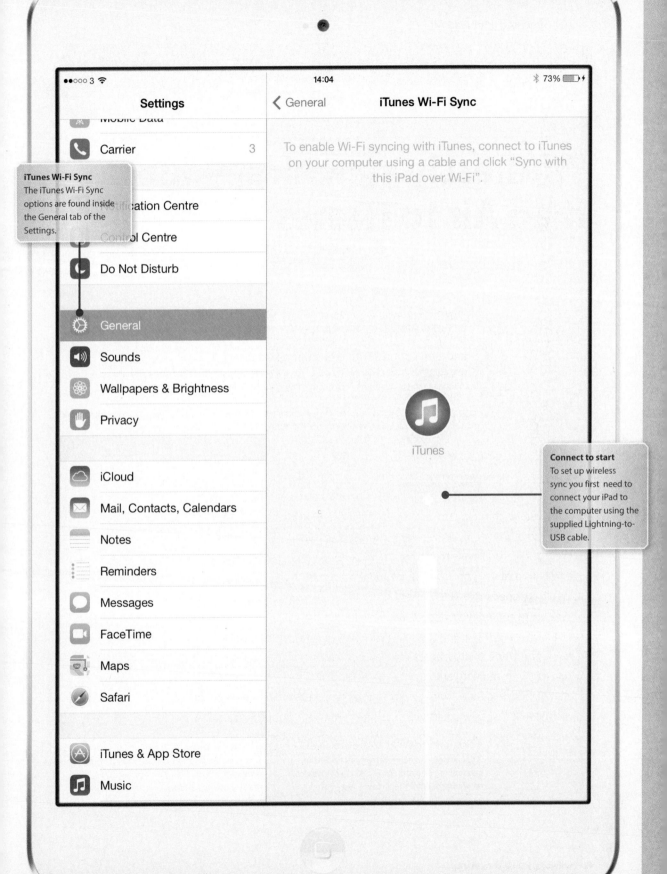

●●○○○ 3 📶   14:04   ✳ 73% 🔋⚡

Settings

‹ General   **iTunes Wi-Fi Sync**

Mobile Data

📞 Carrier   3

iTunes Wi-Fi Sync
The iTunes Wi-Fi Sync options are found inside the General tab of the Settings.

Notification Centre

Control Centre

🌙 Do Not Disturb

⚙️ General

🔊 Sounds

✳️ Wallpapers & Brightness

✋ Privacy

☁️ iCloud

✉️ Mail, Contacts, Calendars

Notes

Reminders

💬 Messages

📷 FaceTime

Maps

🧭 Safari

Ⓐ iTunes & App Store

🎵 Music

To enable Wi-Fi syncing with iTunes, connect to iTunes on your computer using a cable and click "Sync with this iPad over Wi-Fi".

🎵
iTunes

Connect to start
To set up wireless sync you first need to connect your iPad to the computer using the supplied Lightning-to-USB cable.

STEP-BY-STEP GUIDE: Wirelessly synching your iPad Air

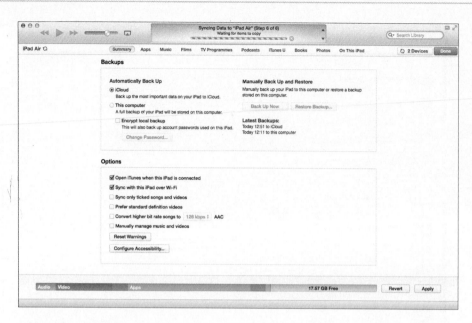

1 Connect your iPad Connect the iPad to your computer using the Lightning cable and open iTunes. Click iPad Air in the top-right (or click Devices then iPad Air, if more than one device is connected).

2 Start Wireless Sync In iTunes, click the Summary tab then, under the Options section, tick the box next to 'Sync With This iPad Over Wi-Fi'. Now click Apply in the iTunes window.

3 Connect to Wi-Fi Make sure the iPad Air is connected to a network by going to Settings and tapping Network, Wi-Fi. Select your wireless network and enter the password if required.

4 Sync wirelessly To ensure that your wireless sync is set up, disconnect your iPad Air from your computer and plug it in to a power source. Open the Settings app and tap on 'iTunes Wi-Fi Sync'.

5 Sync apps With the iPad Air showing in iTunes, click on the Apps tab. Here you can choose which apps to sync to your iPad Air. Click on Install next to the apps you want to add to the iPad.

6 Arrange apps You can rearrange the position of app icons and folders using the Home Screens and individual folder windows to the right. Drag app icons on top of one another to create folders.

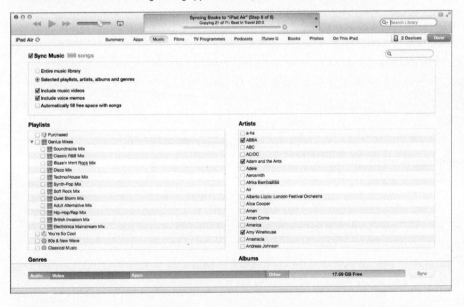

7 Add content Use the Music, Films, TV Programmes and other tabs to decide what other content you want from iTunes to be added to the iPad.

8 Sync it over Keep an eye on the Storage bar at the bottom of the screen. This lets you know how much space is free. Click the Sync button in the bottom right when you are ready to sync items.

Wired first

If you have loads of apps, music, photos and videos to sync to your iPad Air, it's best to do so over USB before going fully wireless. This makes any later syncs much smaller and faster. Once you've got all your stuff synched up, the incremental additions will be smoother.

Setting up and configuring iCloud

Get everything in sync and stored safely online with iCloud

iCLOUD REPLACES THE MOBILEME SERVICE THAT Apple used to offer. This new and improved service is completely free and helps you to keep all your data in sync and backed up with ease. iCloud securely stores all your music, photos, documents and apps and allows you to automatically download them whenever and wherever you are.

KIT LIST:
- IPad
- Apple ID
- Wi-Fi connection

Time required: 10 mins
Difficulty: Beginner

The best thing about the iCloud service is there's no synching required – everything just happens automatically. Buy an app on your iPad Air, for example, and it's automatically sent to your iPhone. Similarly, if you download a new album on your iPhone, it's ready and waiting for you on your iPad Air. It works seamlessly and invisibly in the background.

It's not just for music and apps, though, as iCloud ensures that your email, contacts and calendars are all kept up to date, too. It doesn't matter on which of your devices the change is made, every single one will simply update itself to match when the change is made.

You get 5GB of free storage; since apps, books, music and TV shows don't count toward this space, it's a generous allowance. If you need more space you can buy it. You can also back up your iPad Air to iCloud for an added level of protection. No matter what happens, your data will be safe. iCloud also includes Photo Stream that immediately pushes any pictures you take on your iPad Air to your Mac. There's a lot more to iCloud and it's sure to be greatly expanded in the future. We'll show you how to set it up here.

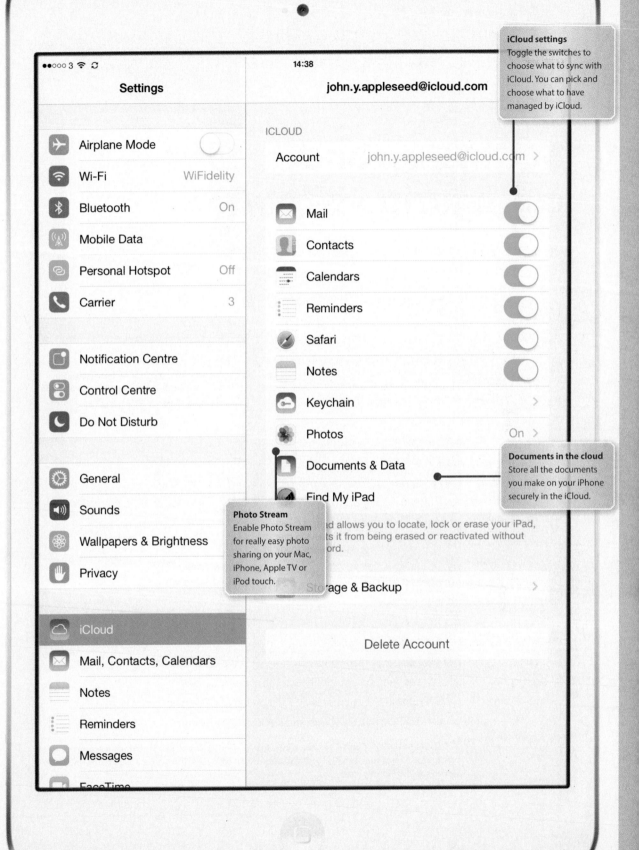

Settings

●●○○○ 3 📶 ⟳

- ✈️ Airplane Mode
- 📶 Wi-Fi — WiFidelity
- ✳️ Bluetooth — On
- 📡 Mobile Data
- ⭕ Personal Hotspot — Off
- 📞 Carrier — 3

- ▦ Notification Centre
- ⬜ Control Centre
- 🌙 Do Not Disturb

- ⚙️ General
- 🔊 Sounds
- 🌸 Wallpapers & Brightness
- ✋ Privacy

- ☁️ iCloud
- ✉️ Mail, Contacts, Calendars
- 📝 Notes
- ▤ Reminders
- 💬 Messages
- FaceTime

14:38

john.y.appleseed@icloud.com

ICLOUD

Account — john.y.appleseed@icloud.com >

- ✉️ Mail ⬤
- 👤 Contacts ⬤
- ▦ Calendars ⬤
- ▤ Reminders ⬤
- 🧭 Safari ⬤
- 📝 Notes ⬤
- 🔑 Keychain >
- 🌸 Photos — On >
- 📄 Documents & Data
- Find My iPad

d allows you to locate, lock or erase your iPad,
ts it from being erased or reactivated without
ord.

Storage & Backup >

Delete Account

iCloud settings
Toggle the switches to choose what to sync with iCloud. You can pick and choose what to have managed by iCloud.

Documents in the cloud
Store all the documents you make on your iPhone securely in the iCloud.

Photo Stream
Enable Photo Stream for really easy photo sharing on your Mac, iPhone, Apple TV or iPod touch.

STEP-BY-STEP GUIDE: Setting up iCloud

1 Get an Apple ID If you don't already have an Apple ID then you'll need to create a new one. Tap on Settings then select iCloud. From here, tap on 'Create A Free Apple ID'.

2 New ID You can use an existing email address or get a new @me.com one for free. Enter your birthday, first and last names and choose an Apple ID (which will also be your iCloud email address).

3 iCloud settings Click Ok to Allow iCloud to sync the location of your iPad. This will help with services such as Find My iPad.

4 Find My iPad Should you lose your iPad, the Find My iPad function of iCloud will be invaluable. Make sure it's turned on and you'll be able to locate your iPad any time, anywhere.

5 **Storage capacity** To see how much of your 5GB data allowance you are using simply tap on 'Storage & Backup'. Here you'll see how much is left for your documents, photos and settings.

6 **Get more space** If 5GB isn't enough storage, you can buy more iCloud space. It's available in 10-, 20- and 50GB portions and costs £14, £28 and £70 per year respectively.

Photo Stream
If you want to share your pictures easily, turn on the Photo Stream part of iCloud. This lets you share up to 1,000 photos between an iPad, iPhone, iPod touch, Apple TV and your Mac. As soon as you take a picture with your iPhone, it's put in your Photo Stream.

7 **Documents & Data** Some iPad apps use the iCloud service to store any documents and data saved in them. Tap 'Storage & Backup', Manage Storage to see which apps are using iCloud.

8 **iCloud Backup** You can use your iCloud storage space as a backup location for all your data. Tap 'Storage & Backup' and set iCloud Backup to On. Tap Ok to start backing up your iPad to iCloud.

Setting up email accounts on your iPad Air

Configure your iPad to send and receive email

EVEN IN THIS AGE OF SOCIAL MEDIA AND TEXTING, email remains the main way that people keep in touch. The iPad is a powerful device for messaging. Its large screen and onscreen keyboard make it easy to read, and send, email messages. And it's always listening for new email messages, thanks to the permanent internet connection and long-lasting battery.

KIT LIST:
- iPad
- Email accounts
- Apple ID

Time required: 10 mins
Difficulty: Intermediate

When you set up the iPad for the first time you should get an Apple ID. This will be a name followed by '@icloud.com'. This is one email account you'll find easy to use, because it's part of your iPad and will be added to the iPad when you first set up the device (See *Setting up your iPad for the first time*, page 40). You can use this to send and receive emails from your iPad, as well as from other computers and Apple's online iCloud web service (icloud.com).

Many people use other email services such as Gmail and Microsoft Exchange. These can be quickly added to the iPad, and you can then send and receive email from these accounts, too. You can add as many different email accounts as you want to an iPad, even multiple accounts from the same service (you can add more than one iCloud and Gmail account to the iPad). These accounts can send and receive mail, and are also used to sync Contacts, Calendars and Reminders across devices. You can use Google to sync calendars instead of iCloud if you want.

This tutorial will show you how to add multiple email accounts to your iPad so you can view and send all your emails from one place.

▶

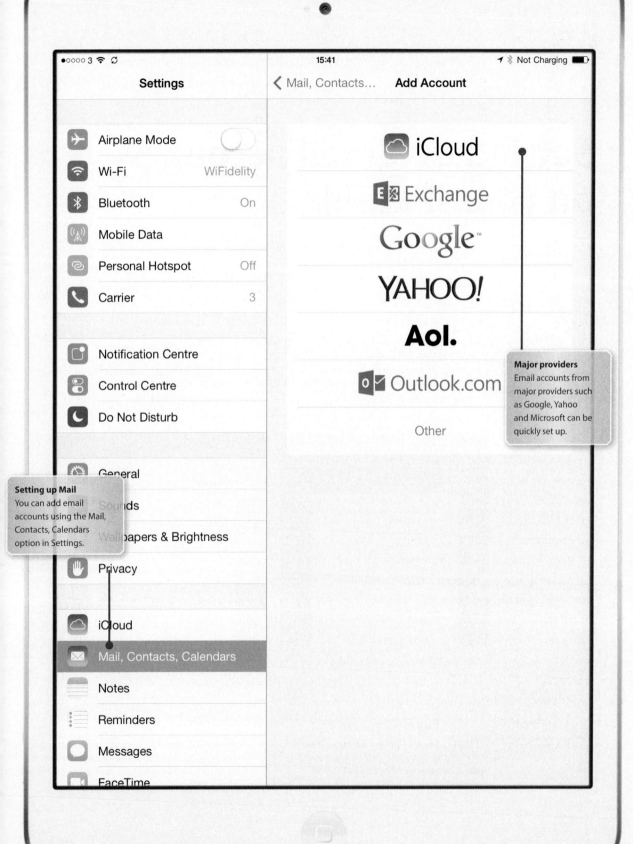

●○○○○ 3 📶 🔄   15:41   ➤ ✳ Not Charging ▪️▪️▪️

Settings   ‹ Mail, Contacts...   **Add Account**

✈️ Airplane Mode	⚪
📶 Wi-Fi	WiFidelity
✳️ Bluetooth	On
🔺 Mobile Data	
➰ Personal Hotspot	Off
📞 Carrier	3

☁️ iCloud

E✳ Exchange

Google™

YAHOO!

Aol.

o✉ Outlook.com

Other

📋 Notification Centre

🎛️ Control Centre

🌙 Do Not Disturb

⚙️ General

Major providers
Email accounts from
major providers such
as Google, Yahoo
and Microsoft can be
quickly set up.

Setting up Mail
You can add email
accounts using the Mail,
Contacts, Calendars
option in Settings.

Sounds

Wallpapers & Brightness

✋ Privacy

☁️ iCloud

✉️ Mail, Contacts, Calendars

📝 Notes

📋 Reminders

💬 Messages

🎥 FaceTime

STEP-BY-STEP GUIDE: Setting up Mail

1 Open settings Tap on the Settings icon on the Home screen, then 'Mail, Contacts, Calendars' in the sidebar to the left. All your accounts will appear at the top, with options for Mail below.

2 Adding an account Tap Add Account to set up an additional account. Options for the main providers will be displayed. We're going to add a Google account so tap Google.

3 Details Fill out the Name, Email and Password fields. The Description field will be automatically entered, but you can change it to something personal. Click Next.

4 Choose your service Most services offer Contacts, Calendars and Notes alongside regular email. Select the ones you want to include on your iPad and click Save.

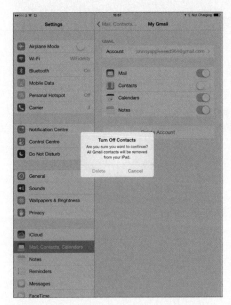

Add signature
You can add a different signature for each email account. Tap on Add Signature, Per Account to access a text field for each account. The text for the signature will be added to the bottom of every email you send.

5 Turn off services It's less confusing to use just one service for your Contacts, Calendars and Notes. You can turn on or off services by tapping them in the 'Mail, Contacts & Calendars' settings and toggling the green On/Off controls.

6 Default account If you have more than one email account you will need to set one account as the default (this is the one used when sending photos, for example). Tap Default Account and select the one you want to use.

7 Mailboxes Open the Mail app and tap on 'All Inboxes and Mailboxes' at the top-left. This will show all the email accounts; you can pick and individual account or view them all.

8 Choose an account When you are creating a new email message, tap the email address in the From field to see a list of your accounts. You can then change the one you want to use.

Set up and use Facebook on your iPad Air

Installing and using Facebook on your iPad is easy

FACEBOOK IS, FOR THE FEW WHO DON'T KNOW, a social-networking site with immense popularity. Almost everyone is on Facebook and it's great for keeping in touch with your friends and family.

Facebook, along with Twitter, Flickr and Vimeo, is one of the few external services that has seen deep iOS integration. You enter your Facebook username and password into the Settings of your iPad, and can then use it to post and share pictures with the social-networking site. You don't even need to download a Facebook app (although you are prompted to and it's better with it installed).

Setting up Facebook is very simple. You can use an account that you already have or create a brand-new one.

The Facebook integration with the iPad is fully complete and, once it is set up, you can use Siri to post a message, and share web pages from Safari or pictures from the Photos app. Your Facebook account is connected to the Settings of the iPad itself.

Another advantage of having Facebook built right into the system is that other apps such as Calendar and Contacts are much more easily able to integrate your account. So your Facebook events will appear in Calendar, and you can sync your Contacts with your Facebook information.

Learn more about Facebook on the iPad Air right here.

KIT LIST:
- iPad
- Facebook account
- Internet connection

Time required: 5 mins
Difficulty: Easy

Settings

Reminders

Messages

FaceTime

Maps

Safari

iTunes & App Store

Music

Videos

Photos & Camera

Books

Podcasts

iTunes U

Game Center

Twitter

Facebook

Flickr

Vimeo

4oD

Access

09:45

Facebook

Facebook
Facebook Inc.

INSTALL

Username   email@example.com

Password   Required

Sign In

Create New Account

Facebook helps you connect and share with people in your life.

Learn More about Facebook

Setting up
You can easily install the standalone Facebook app if you haven't already. Just go to Settings, then tap on Facebook.

Username and password
If you have a Facebook account, enter the details here to integrate iOS and Facebook.

New account
If you aren't tweeting just yet, you can set up an account from within the Settings app. Simply tap 'Create New Account'.

STEP-BY-STEP GUIDE: Set up Facebook

1 Facebook built-in To get started with Facebook on the iPad Air tap on Settings, Facebook in the Sidebar. Enter your username and password, then tap Sign In.

2 New account If you've never set up a Facebook account you can do so within the Settings. Tap on 'Create New Account', fill in the fields, then tap Next. Follow the instructions.

3 Integrated apps Once you've signed in you will see apps connected to your account. Tap 'Update All Contacts' to import your Facebook contact information into your iPad's Contacts app.

4 Install Facebook Tap on Install in Facebook Settings to get the Facebook app from the App Store. You may have to enter your Apple ID and password (not your Facebook password).

5 Log into Facebook The first time you open the Facebook app you will see this screen. It should have your details from the Settings app, so all you need to do is tap Continue.

6 Reading your News Feed The Facebook app works much like the website. You can find friends, view their status updates, and 'Like' and comment on stories.

Twitter

Twitter is a fast-paced social networking site that limits messages to 140 characters. You can set it up in iOS settings by follow the same steps here as Facebook.

7 Posting your events You can post to Facebook from the app by tapping Status. Now write your message and tap Post. You can also use Siri to post to Facebook.

8 Sharing photos You can share images, web pages and other items via Facebook. tap the Share icon in the bottom-left and Facebook. Enter a message and tap Po

Finding information with Siri, your voice assistant

Chat to your iPad and get all the information you need with Siri

THERE'S NO DOUBT THAT THE FEATURE THAT impresses a lot of people with an iPad is Siri, Apple's amazing voice-activated assistant. However, there's a lot more to the Siri than initially meets the eye.

As if Siri wasn't impressive enough at sending dictated messages, you can also use it to perform a host of other tasks. One of the most impressive is how you can use it to find out things. Much like the computers you see in science-fiction, such as *Star Trek* or *2001: A Space Odyssey*, Siri uses natural language to communicate.

It used to be the case that Siri could search for business information only in the US, but the latest update has brought a wealth of business, sports, movie and general trivia information to Siri users in the UK, and iPad Air owners can access all of this at a touch of the Home button.

Answers to basic questions such as 'how many litres in a gallon?' is provided through a link with Wolfram Alpha. But thanks to some of the other technologies built into the iPad, you can use it for other information as well. For instance, if you use the Find My Friends service, you can ask Siri where is one of your contacts and it will show you where they are. Want to know what the weather is like anywhere in the world? Siri can tell you.

This tutorial will show you exactly how to get the most out of Siri and what sort of questions you can ask.

KIT LIST:
- iPad
- Internet connection
- Questions to ask

Time required: 10 mins
Difficulty: Beginner

What can I help you with?

If you don't ask…
Siri can answer all kinds of questions, and help you add all sorts of information to the iPad.

What to say?
Tapping this Help icon brings up a list of all the sorts of things you can ask Siri.

Hold to talk
Hold down the Home Button to activate Siri. You can talk to Siri at any time on the iPad.

STEP-BY-STEP GUIDE: Get info with Siri

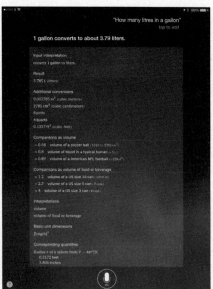

1 Just ask Siri is great for finding out little titbits of information you might need to know. Hold down the Home button to activate Siri, then just ask your question out loud.

2 Answers Siri uses Wolfram Alpha and Bing to find many of its answers; this can be useful for extra context and information. It will often provide the answer plus a lot of detailed information.

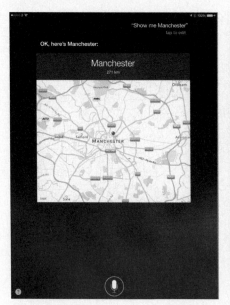

3 Find places You can get Siri to check and find places on the Maps app, either by looking for entire locations or postcodes, or even people using Find My Friends.

4 Siri is in business Siri now searches for businesses in the UK, so if you ask for the nearest Starbucks this is what you're going to see. Click an option to open it in Maps.

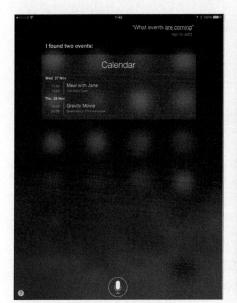

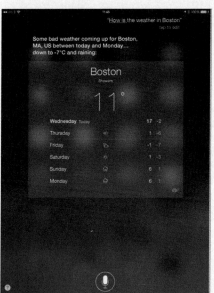

5 Next event Want to know when your next calendar event is? Just ask Siri. Your next appointment will be displayed. To find out whether you have a meeting on a specific date, ask Siri.

6 The weather Want to know what the weather is like in a certain place? Just ask. If you have Local Weather turned on in the Weather app ask 'will it rain tomorrow?' and Siri will tell you.

Speak normally

You can use natural language to ask Siri to find the information you're after – it usually works out what you want to know.

7 Search for sport In addition to all the clever stuff Siri can do, it can also provide the latest sport information. Ask Siri what happened in the latest match to get the results.

8 Siri suggestions If you can't think of anything to ask Siri there are some handy built-in suggestions to get you started. Launch Siri and tap the Help ('?') button for some examples.

Quickly access features with Control Centre

Quickly access key features on your iPad Air

CONTROL CENTRE IS A NEW FEATURE INTRODUCED in iOS 7. It replaces the old Multitasking bar controls and offers a huge range of features.

You access the Control Centre by dragging your finger up from the bottom of the display. The controls pull in like a transparent overlay covering the home screen or whatever app you have open. You can open Control Centre in pretty much any app or part of the iPad. Some apps that rely on similar gestures, such as maps and games, may require you to swipe up twice: once to reveal the handle for Control Centre, and a second time to reveal Control Centre.

One thing that's worth noting is that you can access Control Centre from the Lock screen, although you have to drag your finger up from the very middle of the screen (just above the Home button). If you drag up from the side of the display you'll access the camera instead.

Control Centre can be a bit daunting at first. Don't worry, though, this tutorial will explain how it all works.

The Control Centre is divided into five main parts. These enable you to access Settings, Brightness, Music controls, AirDrop and AirPlay and shortcuts to apps and features.

Control Centre is an incredibly useful new feature on the iPad. This tutorial will help you get started.

KIT LIST:
- iPad
- Internet connection

Time required: 5 mins
Difficulty: Beginner

▶

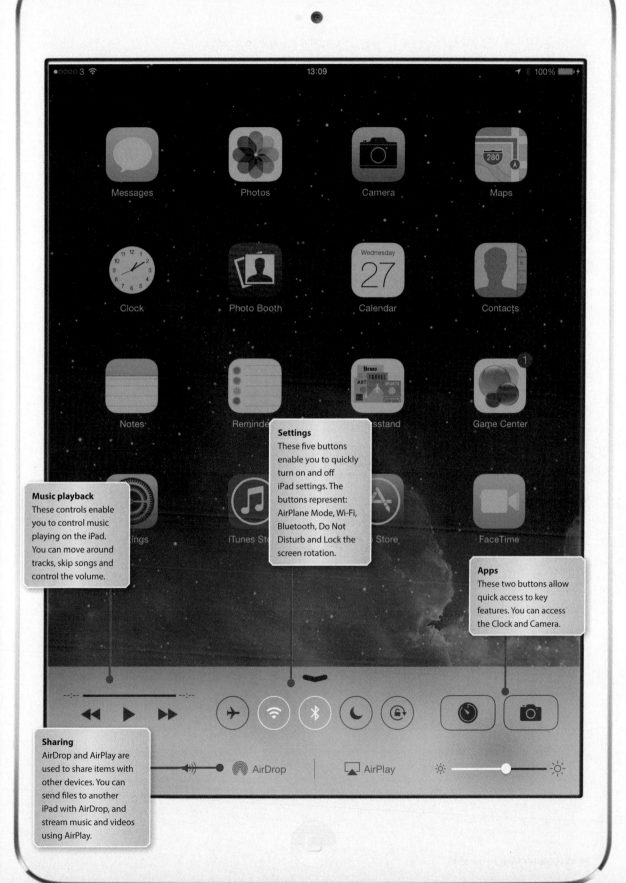

Music playback
These controls enable you to control music playing on the iPad. You can move around tracks, skip songs and control the volume.

Settings
These five buttons enable you to quickly turn on and off iPad settings. The buttons represent: AirPlane Mode, Wi-Fi, Bluetooth, Do Not Disturb and Lock the screen rotation.

Apps
These two buttons allow quick access to key features. You can access the Clock and Camera.

Sharing
AirDrop and AirPlay are used to share items with other devices. You can send files to another iPad with AirDrop, and stream music and videos using AirPlay.

STEP-BY-STEP GUIDE: Control Centre

1 Control Centre Drag your finger upward from the bottom of the display to reveal the Control Centre. It's usually best to start from ever so slightly below the screen.

2 Settings You can turn on settings using the round buttons in the middle. When a feature is active it will turn white. Do Not Disturb and Screen Lock are handy to turn on and off.

3 Brightness The slider at the bottom-right is used to control screen brightness. Drag it down to dim the screen and extend battery life. Drag it to the right to make the screen brighter.

4 Music When music is playing you'll see the name of the track on the left. You can play/pause or skip to the next track and control the playback and volume using the surrounding controls.

5 Open app You can go to the Music app by tapping the name of the song in the middle. Drag Control Centre up from the bottom again to reveal the onscreen controls.

6 AirDrop This is a new feature that enables you to share files with other users nearby. You can share with everybody or just people in your contacts. Tap AirDrop to get started.

Portrait mode
On the Home screen the Control Centre opens vertically, so you may think it works only in portrait mode. This isn't the case. You can open Control Centre in landscape mode by dragging up from the bottom of the display.

7 Quick apps The buttons on the left of the Control Centre offer quick access to apps. Tap the Clock icon to go straight to that app.

8 Open everywhere You can access Control Centre from anywhere. It works on top of apps – for example, here it is displayed over Maps.

Getting to grips with Notification Centre

Notification Centre is the perfect way to see your alerts and messages

PREVIOUS VERSIONS OF iOS NOTIFICATIONS COULD become a bit of a pain. The single-message windows that popped up and interrupted whatever you were doing were distracting. Halfway through reading a web page it would suddenly pause and you'd get a message that someone had just checked in on Foursquare, or that you'd been mentioned on Twitter.

KIT LIST:
- iPad
- Internet connection

Time required: 5 mins
Difficulty: Beginner

Not to mention that if you had a lot of apps with notifications it could take ages to wade through and dismiss them all. It made using your iPad a bit of a pain, if we're honest. With Notification Centre and iOS 7 all this has changed and now your iPad experience is much more streamlined.

The Notification Centre lets you see far more detail about exactly what's going on, and you can get to it from anywhere at any time. You can happily continue to do what you were doing, be that watching a movie, playing a game or editing a document, and your other apps won't get in the way.

You still get to see what notifications are coming in, but it's on your terms. The Notification Centre doesn't have to be restricted to standard messages, though. It will display the weather forecast and – if you're interested – stock prices, too. All the notifications are kept hidden away until you need them.

This tutorial will show you how to take a look at all your alerts using the new Notification Centre features.

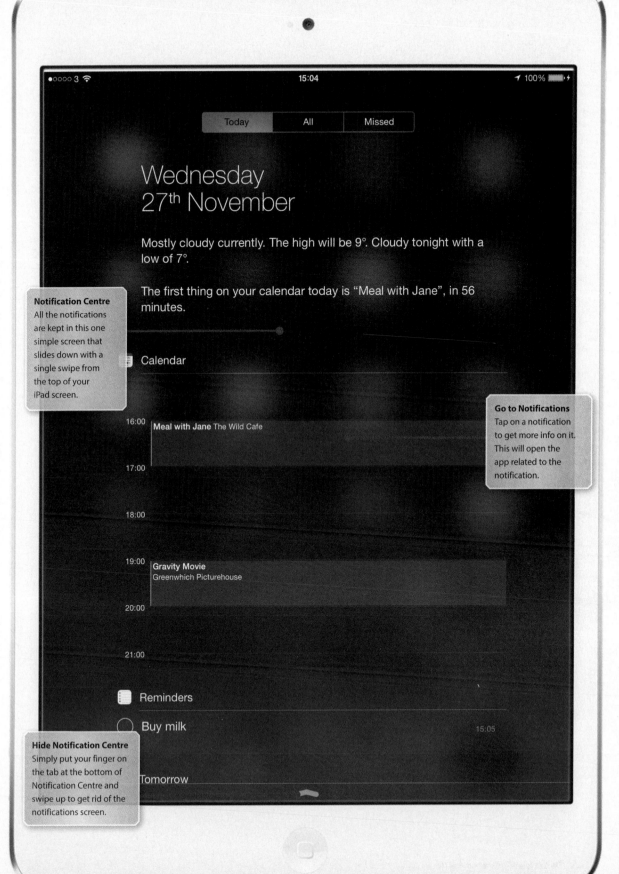

●○○○○ 3 📶   15:04   ⬈ 100% ▬▬▬ ⚡

| Today | All | Missed |

Wednesday
27ᵗʰ November

Mostly cloudy currently. The high will be 9°. Cloudy tonight with a low of 7°.

The first thing on your calendar today is "Meal with Jane", in 56 minutes.

Notification Centre
All the notifications are kept in this one simple screen that slides down with a single swipe from the top of your iPad screen.

Calendar

Go to Notifications
Tap on a notification to get more info on it. This will open the app related to the notification.

16:00   **Meal with Jane** The Wild Cafe

17:00

18:00

19:00   **Gravity Movie**
Greenwhich Picturehouse

20:00

21:00

Reminders

Buy milk   15:05

Hide Notification Centre
Simply put your finger on the tab at the bottom of Notification Centre and swipe up to get rid of the notifications screen.

Tomorrow

STEP-BY-STEP GUIDE: Notification Centre

1 **Home screen** One of the big advantages of the Notification Centre is updates are displayed almost everywhere. Here we can see that somebody has sent us a Mail message.

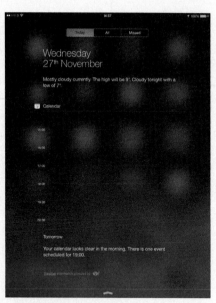

2 **Notification Centre** To get to the Notification Centre itself you simply swipe down the screen with your fingertip, from the very top of the screen to the bottom, in one fluid movement.

3 **Today and All** The default Today view shows weather, calendar events and reminders. Tap the All button to see all the notifications, including those from apps you have installed.

4 **Missed alerts** Tapping on the Missed button displays all the alerts you didn't spot. This is a good way to see anything you've missed.

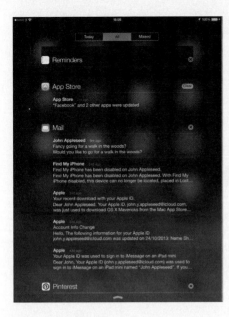

5 Clear notifications In the All view there are lots of notifications from multiple apps. You can clear some space by tapping the Delete ('X') icon and then Clear.

6 Scroll down Swipe down to see more of your messages and notifications. If you install a lot of apps you'll find the All window starts to fill up with notifications.

7 More detail If you want to get more detail on any of the items in Notification Centre, simply tap on an alert to be taken to the relevant app. Here we tapped on an app update.

8 Instant alerts Your notifications will appear even when you're looking at the Home screen. So, no matter what you're doing, you'll always get those important messages.

Badges

If you like the old style of pop-up alerts and badges, you can still see those red badges to alert you to any activity, such as text messages, emails and missed calls. Tap on Settings > Notification Centre, then tap on the app under Include and set 'Badge App Icon' to On.

Managing your notification settings

Keep yourself in charge of what notifications you get from each app

THE ADVANTAGE OF NOTIFICATION CENTRE IN iOS is that all alerts are kept in one place. It's a simple, easy-to-access part of the iPad operating system that makes getting messages and notifications supremely easy. Swipe your finger down the screen and there they all are.

With the addition of iCloud support you can easily see all your appointments and mail in one place. Text messages or iMessages can all be read and assessed for importance at a glance. In short, it's a truly effective way of seeing all your updates in one simple screen.

The only problem with this approach, however, is there are so many apps that want to send you alerts and notifications that the Notification Centre itself can become overwhelmed. Too much information to scroll through and the usefulness of iOS' Notification Centre is gone.

Happily, you can manage how your notifications will appear and which apps will be able to use them. Want to use an app, but not allow it to send you notifications? That's not a problem. Even better, you can decide what type of notifications you receive, be they banners or old-style alerts.

The Notification Centre is based entirely around your preferences. Spend a short time following this tutorial and you will get the most from Notification Centre and always get the alerts you want most. Each and every app is configurable to match your specific needs.

KIT LIST:
- iPad with iOS 7
- Apps with notifications

—————————————

Time required: 20 mins
Difficulty: Intermediate

Banner or Alert
You can choose between pop-up window alerts or banners for all of your apps that provide notifications. Choose None to stop alerts for that app.

●●○○○ 3 ⟨令⟩   16:00

Settings   ⟨ Notification Centre   **Messages**

✈ Airplane Mode   ⬭

⟨令⟩ Wi-Fi   WiFidelity 5GHz

✳ Bluetooth   Off

⦿ Mobile Data

⊘ Personal Hotspot   Off

☏ Carrier   3

ALERT STYLE

None   Banners   Alerts

Alerts require an action before proceeding. Banners appear at the top of the screen and go away automatically.

Badge app icons
The app icons on the Home screen can also display notifications as small numbers on the app icon.

...ification Centre

...ntrol Centre

Do Not Disturb

Badge App Icon   ⬤

Alert Sound   Tri-tone >

ALERTS

⚙ General

◀)) Sounds

❀ Wallpapers & Brightness

✋ Privacy

Show in Notification Centre   ⬤

Include   5 Recent Items >

Show on Lock Screen   ⬤

Show alerts on the Lock screen, and in Notification Centre when it is accessed from the Lock screen.

☁ iCloud

✉ Mail, Contacts, Calendars

▤ Notes

Notification Centre
You can prevent items from showing up in Notification Centre. You will still get the Banner or Alert, though.

Show Preview

Show a preview of the message in alerts, Notification Centre.

⁞ Reminders

◯ Messages

Repeat Alerts   Once >

▣ FaceTime

Show Alerts from Everyone   ✓

Show Alerts from My Contacts

STEP-BY-STEP GUIDE: Notification Centre settings

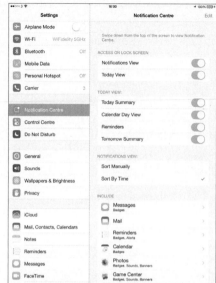

1 Get to notifications To manage your notifications you'll need to go into Settings. Tap on Settings, Notification Centre. Here you will find a variety of settings for complete control.

2 Notification Centre All the applications that use Notification Centre are listed – just swipe up to see more of them. You can choose to have them arranged Manually or By Time.

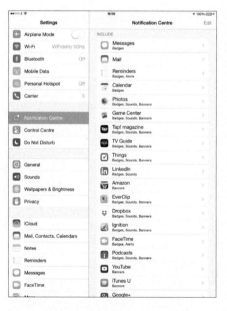

3 Banner or Alert All the apps that appear in Notification Centre appear in the Include section. You can change notification settings for each app. Tap on the name of an app to access its settings.

4 Other notification options Decide whether apps can use a badge, or how often alerts are repeated. You can choose to include or exclude the notification from the iPad lock screen.

5 **Alert repeat** By default, alerts are set to repeat just once. If you often find yourself missing alerts, you can have them repeated up to 10 times so that you never miss a notification.

6 **Show messages** If you want to see more of your messages, simply tap on Recent Items. You can choose to show just 1, 5, 10 or 20 recent items in the list in Notification Centre.

7 **Today view** The Today view is the default window in Notification Centre. It displays a Summary, Calendar, Reminders and Tomorrow Summary. You can turn off these items if you want.

8 **Do not include** If you decide you no longer want an app in Notification Centre, tap on Edit and drag it down (using the three bar icon) to the 'Do Not Include' section.

Notification setup

When you install a new app on your iPad it may ask for your permission to send you updates and notifications. Tap Ok for it to automatically set up notifications or Don't Allow if you don't want it to. You can always edit the settings later.

Using Safari for iPad

Learn how to use gestures and pages in Safari for iPad

 AS WITH APPLE'S DESKTOP COMPUTERS, SAFARI IS the default browser for the iPad – and on this platform it offers the best mobile browsing experience we know. It offers a gestural touch-based interface, with flick-scrolling, pinch-zooming and links that are activated with a tap.

Safari on the iPad Air offers most of the features found on a desktop computer, including support for multiple tabs. Pages are similar to a desktop browser's tabs, enabling you to simultaneously browse multiple sites.

You can also share web pages via email or AirDrop, or add them to a Reading List that downloads pages for offline viewing. There are some unique features, too, such as Shared Links (which shows links to the pages being shared by your friends using social media).

As with its desktop cousin there is a single Smart Search Field at the top, which lets you enter URLs, perform web searches, access bookmarks and even find search terms on a page.

Here we show you how to get started with Safari, working with gestures, pages and special features. Once you start interacting directly with web content on the iPad's screen, you'll be hooked. In fact, you may well find the combination of your computer's browser and a mouse starts to feel rather archaic by comparison. Let's get started with Safari.

KIT LIST:
- iPad
- Internet connection

Time required: 5 mins
Difficulty: Beginner

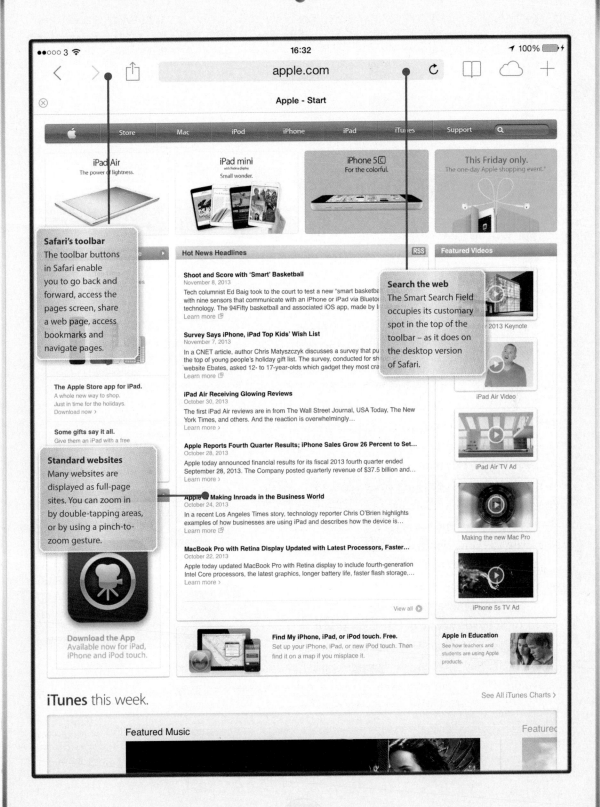

Safari's toolbar
The toolbar buttons in Safari enable you to go back and forward, access the pages screen, share a web page, access bookmarks and navigate pages.

Search the web
The Smart Search Field occupies its customary spot in the top of the toolbar – as it does on the desktop version of Safari.

Standard websites
Many websites are displayed as full-page sites. You can zoom in by double-tapping areas, or by using a pinch-to-zoom gesture.

STEP-BY-STEP GUIDE: Getting to know Safari

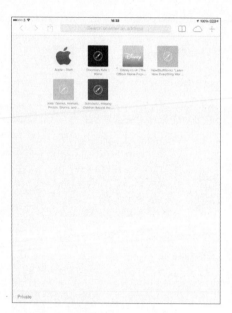

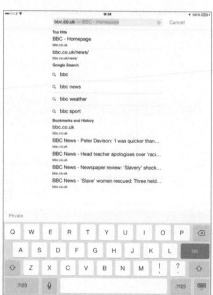

1 Open a web page... When you first open Safari you'll be presented with some bookmarks from your Favourites selection. This is preloaded with some Apple selections. Tap one to view.

2 ...Or search the web To search the web tap the Smart Search Field and enter a search term. Now tap Go. The default Search engine is Google. You can also enter a specific URL and tap Go.

3 Navigate a page You can move around a web page by dragging your finger up and down. You can also move horizontally across a page.

4 Zoom page content If you want to zoom in on an object double-tap it. Safari zooms to fit that text. Or you can use the pinch-to-zoom gesture.

5 Use tabs To view more than one page tap the New Tab ('+') icon. This will open a new blank web page, and you will see tabs appear. Tapping these tabs moves from one page to the other.

6 Bookmarks and sharing Tap the Share icon to share or bookmark a page. You can add it to a Bookmark or your Reading List or create a Home screen icon from the page.

A good turn
Safari for iPad works well in both portrait and landscape orientations. If you find yourself regularly zooming in and out on a certain website, try rotating your iPad to landscape mode – the page will resize accordingly, and the text will be bigger. You will see less of the web page overall, but the effortless scroll-based navigation of Safari means this is unlikely to be a problem.

7 Play video To start playing video tap the play icon at its centre. To access Play and Pause controls tap the video; use the timeline to move through the video. The controls will quickly fade.

8 Go full-screen Tap the fullscreen icon in the bottom right to view a video without the rest of the web page. You can tap it again to return to the web page.

Using Safari Reader and sharing web pages

Safari Reader makes websites and blog posts much easier to read

SAFARI IS ONE OF THE BEST MOBILE WEB browsers, if not the best mobile web browser. The fast and accurate way it renders pages is impressive. The browser is no doubt helped by the super-fast chip inside the iPad Air. With 4G connectivity becoming more commonplace, the faster your browser can render a page the better.

One of the problems with having a smaller screen is some website designs make it difficult to see the content you want to get at. This isn't too much of an issue where you can pinch-to-zoom or double-tap on text to get a closer view, but it can still be a pain.

To get a better view of the main body text on web pages, Apple has included in Safari a feature called Reader. Reader automatically cuts out all the design elements of a page and just gives you the text and key images. Reader is great for longer blog posts and news stories. You can enlarge the text to make it even easier to read, too.

In the Reader view you also have quick access to other sharing options, such as Reading List, Tweet and Print.

The Reader function might not work on every web page, and you'll have to wait for the page to fully load before you can take advantage of it, but it makes reading on the web a much more pleasant experience.

Read on to find out how to get the best out of the Reader feature and make reading online news and blog posts a lot simpler.

KIT LIST:
- iPad
- Web page to share
- Twitter account

Time required: 10 mins
Difficulty: Intermediate

The 3D printer that can build a house in 24 hours

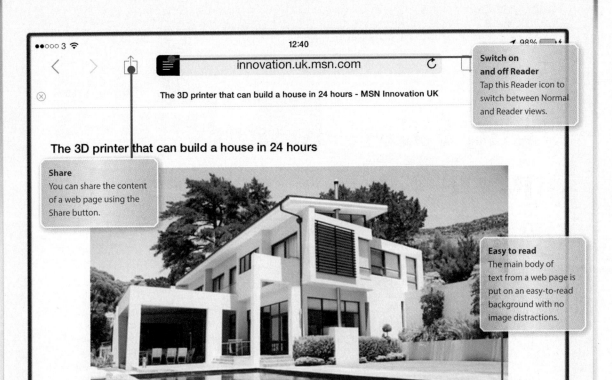

Getty

The University of Southern California is testing a giant 3D printer that could be used to build a whole house in under 24 hours.

Professor Behrokh Khoshnevis has designed the giant robot that replaces construction workers with a nozzle on a gantry, this squirts out concrete and can quickly build a home according to a computer pattern. It is "basically scaling up 3D printing to the scale of building," says Khoshnevis. The technology, known as Contour Crafting, could revolutionise the construction industry.

The affordable home?

Contour Crafting could slash the cost of home-owning, making it possible for millions of displaced people to get on the property ladder. It could even be used in disaster relief areas to build emergency and replacement housing. For example, after an event such as Typhoon Haiyan in the Philippines, which has displaced almost 600,000 people, Contour Crafting could be used to build replacement homes quickly.

It could be used to create high-quality shelter for people currently living in desperate

STEP-BY-STEP GUIDE: **Using Safari Reader**

1 **Basic page** Safari is very good at rendering web pages and the Retina display makes text extra sharp, but it can be easier to read. Tap on Reader in the Address Bar.

2 **Reader view** When you've stripped out all the other web page elements, the article is much easier to read. Any images in the text will still be displayed onscreen.

3 **Links** Pages still contain web links, so you can click on them to access new pages. These open in Normal view, however, but it's a quick process to switch each page to Reader view.

4 **Sharing service** As well as giving you a clearer view of web pages, Reader lets you share a page in a number or ways. Send articles via email or Twitter, or even print them out.

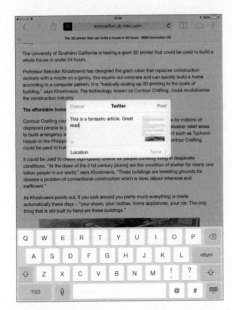

5 Tweet an article
If you use Twitter you can quickly let your followers know about an article, directly from the Reader view. Tap on the Share icon, then Twitter.

6 Email an article
If you're not on Twitter you can still share articles via email. Tap on the Share icon and select Mail, and your link and subject will be automatically filled in.

Navigate
You can navigate forward and backward between Safari pages by sliding your finger in from the left and right of the display. This is much quicker than using the Forward and Back buttons in the Safari toolbar.

7 Shared links
A new feature in Safari enables you to view all the web pages your friends are sharing inside Safari. Tap on Bookmarks and the Shared Links icon to view all pages being shared.

8 Normal view
Once you have read the article you can return to the standard web view to see and read all the elements Reader cut out. Simply tap the Reader icon to switch to Normal view.

Sending and reading email with your iPad

Discover how the iPad's Mail app works

THE iPAD IS A FANTASTIC COMMUNICATION TOOL.
It's small and portable, and almost permanently
connected to the internet. And its large screen makes
reading email a joy. The iPad also makes it incredibly
easy to send and receive email, thanks in part to the
iCloud service that you get along with your Apple
devices. This includes a high-quality email service
that you can use to send and receive messages. These are sent using your
@iCloud.com email address (which is also your Apple ID).

Reading messages that people have sent you couldn't be easier. Just tap
on the Mail app on the Home screen and you can read all your emails. Slide
your finger in from the left of the screen to view all the messages in your
inbox (unread messages will be highlighted with a blue circle). As you tap
each message it appears in the main window (and the highlight disappears
so you know which emails you have read).

You can quickly reply to emails, or create new ones. And because iCloud
is a push email service the messages will be sent immediately, and you'll get
a notification as soon as the other person replies.

Let's get started with Apple Mail.

KIT LIST:
- iPad
- Apple ID
- Person to email

Time required: 10 mins
Difficulty: Beginner

▶

●○○○○ 3 📶   11:10   ⚓ ✳ 74% 🔋

‹ Mailboxes   **Inbox**   Edit   ⚑   🗀   🗑   ↩   ✎

Q Search   Hide

Find My iPhone   10/10/2013
Find My iPhone has been disabled on…
Find My iPhone has been disabled on
John Appleseed. With Find My iPhone…

● **Apple**   09/10/2013
Your Apple ID was used to sign in to i…
Dear John, Your Apple ID
(john.y.appleseed@icloud.com) was u…

● **Apple**   03/10/2013
Your Apple ID was used to sign in to F…   ┌─────────────────────┐
Dear John, Your Apple ID   │ **New message**   │
(john.y.appleseed@icloud.com) was u…   │ Tap this New Message│
                                                        │ icon to start a new │
● **Apple**   30/09/2013   │ email. You can respond│
Your Apple ID was used to sign in to i…   **e to iCloud Mail** │ to emails using the │
Dear John. Your Apple ID   │ Reply button to the left.│
┌──────────────┐ed@icloud.com) was u…   **s john.y.appleseed@icloud.com.** └─────────┘
│ **Inbox**   │
│ All your messages│   ce or computer, turn on Mail in iCloud settings. You can
│ will appear in this│   26/09/2013   ss your mail at iCloud.com.
│ inbox. Those you│ was used to sign in to F…
│ haven't read will be│ r Apple ID
│ highlighted with a│ed@icloud.com) was u…
│ blue circle. │   **iCloud**
└──────────────┘   24/09/2013
Your Apple ID was used to sign in to i…   My Apple ID | Support | Terms and Conditions | Privacy Policy
Dear John, Your Apple ID   33, rue Sainte Zithe, L-2763 Luxembourg. All rights reserved.
(john.y.appleseed@icloud.com) was u…

● **Apple**   23/09/2013
Your Apple ID was used to sign in to i…
Dear John, Your Apple ID
(john.y.appleseed@icloud.com) was u…
                                          ┌──────────────────────┐
iCloud   ●──── 23/09/20   │ **Reading list**   │
Welcome to iCloud Mail.   │ The email that you're│
Your email address is   │ currently reading will have│
john.y.appleseed@icloud.com. To use…   │ this grey highlight. │
                                          └──────────────────────┘
iCloud   23/09/2013
Welcome to iCloud.
Your Apple ID is
john.y.appleseed@icloud.com Now th…

Updated Just Now
16 Unread

STEP-BY-STEP GUIDE: Using Mail

1 Welcome to Mail Tap on the Mail icon on the Home screen to access your email. If you have created an Apple ID and set up iCloud you should already have a welcome message from Apple.

2 View the inbox Messages that people send to your @icloud.com email will appear in the inbox. Slide your finger in from the left of the screen to view the inbox messages).

3 New message You create a new message by tapping the New Message icon in the top right. To the left of this is a Reply button that enables you to respond to people who have emailed you.

4 Enter your message Enter the person's email address using the To field at the top. You should also enter a Subject for the message, and the main text. Tap Send to deliver the email.

5 Inserting photos
You can also add photos and video to your email. To do this tap and hold any part of the main window and let go. This bubble menu will appear. Tap on Insert Photo or Video.

6 Choose your photo
Mail will display all the photos from your Photos app. You can scroll up and down and tap Photos in the top to view your albums. Tap on an image to add it to the email.

Mailboxes
Mail has mailboxes other than the Inbox. It also has Drafts, Sent, Junk and Trash. You can view these by tapping on Mailboxes to the top left of the Inbox.

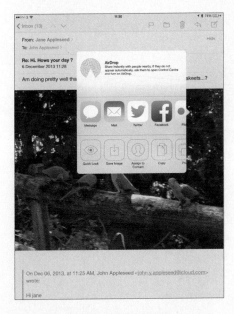

7 Saving images
Photos that other people send to you can be saved to your Photos app. Tap and hold the image to bring up this Share window. Now tap on the Save Image icon.

8 Taking out the Trash
Over time yo... inbox will start to fill up. You can delete unw... messages by sliding your finger across it to t... Now tap on the red Trash icon.

Getting the most from Apple's Messages service

Messages lets you send text and video for free to other iOS devices

WOULDN'T IT BE GREAT IF YOU DIDN'T HAVE TO pay for text messages? Now you don't. iMessage is built into iOS and lets you send free messages to anyone with an iPhone, iPad or iPod touch. You can send pictures and video, as well as plain text messages, provided the recipient has an Apple device. The best part is there's no setup involved. Your iPad will automatically detect whether the recipient has an iDevice and send the message to them using a system Apple calls iMessage, which you access using the Messages app. There's often some confusion between the two: Messages is the App you use, iMessage is the name of the service that sends free messages to other iOS devices. So The Messages app can send iMessages (and also SMS text messages on the iPhone, but not on the iPad).

You can send group messages, so if you need to let everyone in the family know what's going on, just add them to the conversation and type away. You can see when the other person is typing a reply and there are delivery and read receipts so that you know when your message got through.

All the messages are encrypted with the latest security software, so there's no chance your conversations can be read by anyone else. Also, thanks to the new voice-recognition system, you can dictate messages direct to your iPad. This makes sending those short messages even faster, and it's surprisingly accurate, too. Don't worry though, you can still use the keyboard if talking to your phone makes you feel a little bit self-conscious.

KIT LIST:
- iPad
- Contacts with iOS devices
- Internet connection

Time required: 5 mins
Difficulty: Beginner

▷

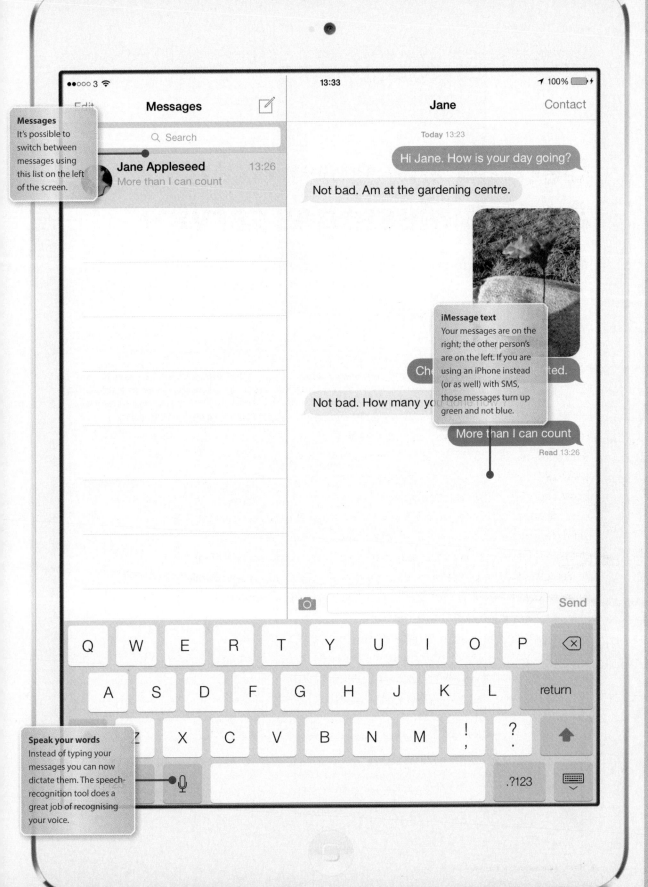

STEP-BY-STEP GUIDE: Setting up and using Messages

1 Make a message The Messages app can send text messages to other iOS devices. Tap on the new message icon on the Home screen and enter your Apple ID and Password. Now tap Sign In.

2 Spot iMessage users As you begin to type, your contacts show up below the To field. Contacts who are also iMessage users will appear in blue. You can send texts to these people.

3 Write a message Simply tap on the name of the contact you want to message and start to type. Tap the blue Send button to fire off your message to the other person.

4 iOS only On the iPad you can only send Messages to other people using iMessage. On the iPhone you can use SMS as well. So bear in mind your non-iOS owning friends.

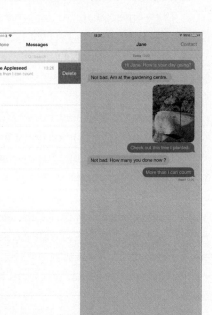

5 Picture message If you want to send a picture, just tap on the camera icon. Here you can choose an image from your library or take a new picture with the iPad's camera.

6 See the response When the other person is typing a response you can see it in the chat window. The speech bubble with three dots indicates that the other person is writing a reply.

Read receipts
If you want people to know for certain that you've read their message, you can switch on read receipts. Enable these receipts in the Settings app.

7 Speak your messages Instead of typing messages you can dictate them. Tap the microphone button and speak. Then tap Done. The iPad turns your speech into text.

8 Clear your messages Over time you're likely to get hundreds of messages. You can delete conversations in the Messages app. Swipe across the message from right to left and then tap Delete.

Sending emails and text messages with Siri

Siri understands spoken commands and can perform many tasks

SIRI IS ONE OF THE MOST OUTSTANDING FEATURES of the iPad. Siri can understand your voice and act upon your instructions. It's not just simple voice recognition, however: you can get Siri to perform all manner of tasks. Apple is keen to point out Siri isn't a completely foolproof system, but it's pretty good.

There are some restrictions that mean Siri can't always work. You have to have a 3G/4G or Wi-Fi data connection to use the service. If you can't connect, Siri just won't be able to do anything. This is because it needs to connect to Apple's servers for help with turning your voice into instructions.

It might seem a bit odd talking to your iPad, but when you get used to doing so it seems perfectly normal. If you still find it uncomfortable speaking to your iPad you can use the headphones to make Siri work. There have been a lot of examples of the fun you can have with Siri, but it can do some really interesting and useful things, too.

On of Siri's coolest features is the ability to dictate and send messages to your contacts. You can use email or text, and all you have to do is open Siri and ask it to send a message. It's a lot easier than typing out messages by hand. This easy-to-follow tutorial shows you exactly how to start sending messages with Siri.

KIT LIST:
- iPad
- Apple ID
- Friend on iMessage

Time required: 15 mins
Difficulty: Intermediate

What can I help you with?

Interaction
Siri speaks back to you, and its responses appear on the main display. Sometimes you can click on options in this window as well as speak to Siri.

Voice indicator
The horizontal waveform indicates when Siri is hearing. It spins when Siri is thinking and turns into a microphone icon. You can tap this to tell Siri to listen up.

Speak to Siri
Launch Siri with a long press on the Home button, then simply start to speak. If it can help, it will.

1 Send an email To get started sending an email open Siri and say "Send an email." Siri will process the instruction and ask you to whom you want to send a message.

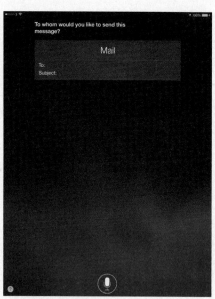

2 Multiple accounts Tell Siri the name of the intended recipient of your email; if you have multiple addresses for that person, Siri will ask which one to use. Speak or tap on your selection.

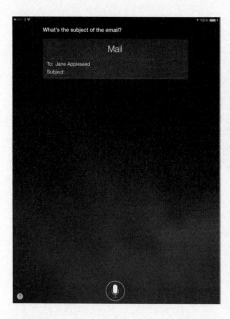

3 Subject matter Siri now asks you for the subject line for your email. Again, all you have to do is speak and Siri will turn your speech to text. Stop speaking to continue (or tap the Siri button).

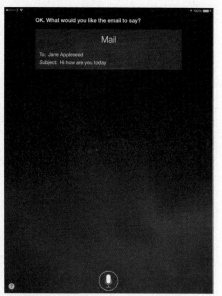

4 Message body All you have to do is dictate your message. Remember to use punctuation. If you want a comma, for example, say "comma". Just stop speaking to continue with Siri.

5 Send email When you're done Siri will ask if you want to send the message. Simply confirm with "Yes" to send the message or "Cancel" to delete it. To change the email say "Change".

6 Send a text message Open Siri and tell it you'd like to send a text message. You can either give Siri a name or it will ask you to whom the message should be sent.

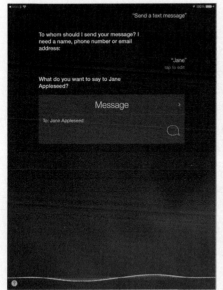

7 Dictate message Speak your message and Siri will turn your speech into words. It will then ask you whether it's okay to send the message. Say "Yes" or "No" as appropriate.

8 Message sent Once you've approved the message Siri will send the text to your contact. Siri is a great alternative to using the keyboard when sending emails and messages.

Natural voice

Give Siri simple instructions and it will interpret each step and ask you the next relevant question. However, it's possible to give Siri a string of instructions. You could say "Send a message to Joanne's work email address" and Siri will know what you mean.

Using Contacts to view and edit your address book

How to search, view and edit contacts on your iPad

LIKE ITS MAC EQUIVALENT, CONTACTS FOR iPAD IS a simple application, relying largely on data you send it via an iTunes or - increasingly - iCloud. Contacts can also be synchronised with a variety of services (including Google Contacts and Yahoo Address Book), along with information from Address Book for Mac OS X and Outlook 2003 or 2007 for Windows.

It's possible to add new contacts (which can, of course, later be sent back to your computer the next time you do a sync), and you can edit details for existing contacts, updating data and creating new fields.

It's also possible to amend the sort order of your contacts. If you prefer the list order to be based on first names rather than surnames, select Mail, Contacts, Calendars in the Settings app and set Sort Order to First, Last. Note that you can also amend a second option, Display Order, to Last, First. This makes names in the app (both in the contacts list and individual contact pages) display as 'Jobs Steve' rather than 'Steve Jobs'. Neither of these options is permanent; if you want to revert to the default setting, simply go to the Settings app and reselect it.

Having a good Contacts list on the iPad makes the whole experience much better, the contacts appear in your emails and messages, and integrate with other apps such as Twitter and Facebook. You can also use them with apps such as Find My Friends, so it's a good idea to keep Contacts up to date.

KIT LIST:
- iPad
- Contact details
- Photo of person

Time required: 20 mins
Difficulty: Intermediate

Search field
The search field in the Contacts app dynamically filters your contacts list, updating as you type.

Add new contact
Click this '+' icon to add a new person or company to the list of entries in Contacts.

14:39   100%

All Contacts   +

Search   Jane Appleseed

A

Apple Inc.

Jane **Appleseed**   home
                                  020 5551 2345
John **Appleseed**
                                  work
Kate **Appleseed**   07555 12345

Nathanial **Appleseed**   home
                                  jane.y.appleseed@icloud.com
Robert **Appleseed**
                                  birthday
                                  24 September 1974

                                  Notes

List of contacts
Contacts appear in a list that you can scroll up and down. Click the letters on the right to go to those alphabetical entries.

                                  Send Message

                                  Share Contact

A
B
C
D
E
F
G
H
I
J
K
L
M
N
O
P
Q
R
S
T
U
V
W
X
Y
Z
#

STEP-BY-STEP GUIDE: **Managing a contacts list**

1 Find a contact Open a contact's page by selecting it from the list. Tap the letters on the left to snap to names, or drag/flick to manually scroll the list.

2 See details A contact's details appear in the righthand side of the window. If the details are too long to be displayed, a scrollbar will briefly appear to signify this.

3 Edit details Tap the Edit button to amend information. Remove fields by tapping the red buttons, then tapping Delete.

4 Removing a contact Scroll to the bottom of the page and tap Delete Contact. In the pop-up dialog tap Delete to confirm, otherwise Cancel.

5 Forward a contact Tap Share Contact to bring up the Share window. You can share it with a person using AirDrop, or via Mail or Message.

6 Add a new contact To start, tap the Add (+) button at the top of the contacts list. A New Contact page will appear.

More fields
To add specific details for a contact when in edit mode, scroll down and tap add field. This brings up a pop-up menu, enabling you to select a new field such as Birthday or Job Title. It's also possible to amend a field's type by selecting it while editing – for example, tap a telephone field to change it from home or work to Skype, iChat or some other option.

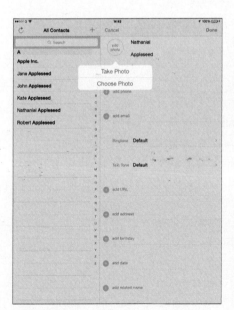

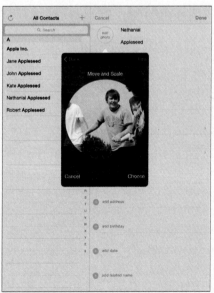

7 Add a photo Adding photos to contacts makes the iPad much better. Tap add photo and either Take Photo or Choose Photo from the menu.

8 Edit photos You can drag and pinch to scale the image, and drag it around using your finger to focus on the face. Tap Choose when you're happy.

Adding and editing events in the Calendar app

Define locations, times, alerts and notes for events

Tuesday

9

THE iPAD HAS A FANTASTIC CALENDAR APP THAT is much more powerful than those you'd use on other tablets. It becomes especially useful if you hook it up to other iOS devices and your computer using Apple's free iCloud synchronisation service.

However, the iPad's Calendar app isn't reliant on being physically synched with a computer. You can add new events and amend existing ones on your iPad. These are then sent over Wi-Fi using iCloud to your other iOS devices – no computer is required.

The process for adding a new event from scratch is pretty straightforward but, when it comes to editing events, it's worth noting one of the options in the Mail, Contacts, Calendars section of the Settings app. Scroll down to Calendars and you'll find the Default Calendar option. Tap this to see a list of the calendars on your iPad. Select one of them and it will be used as the default in the Calendars app when you create a new event. The setting can be overridden on a per-event basis, but it's a good timesaver to have your most-used calendar as the default option.

You can view your calendar by day, week, month or year. In Month view you see all the days and can scroll up and down between months. In Year view you don't get to view any events, but can tap on any month you want to view. In the bottom-left is a Today button that's also worth getting to know. Calendars is a fantastic organiser. Let's take a look at how it works.

KIT LIST:

■ **iPad**

Time required: 5 mins
Difficulty: Beginner

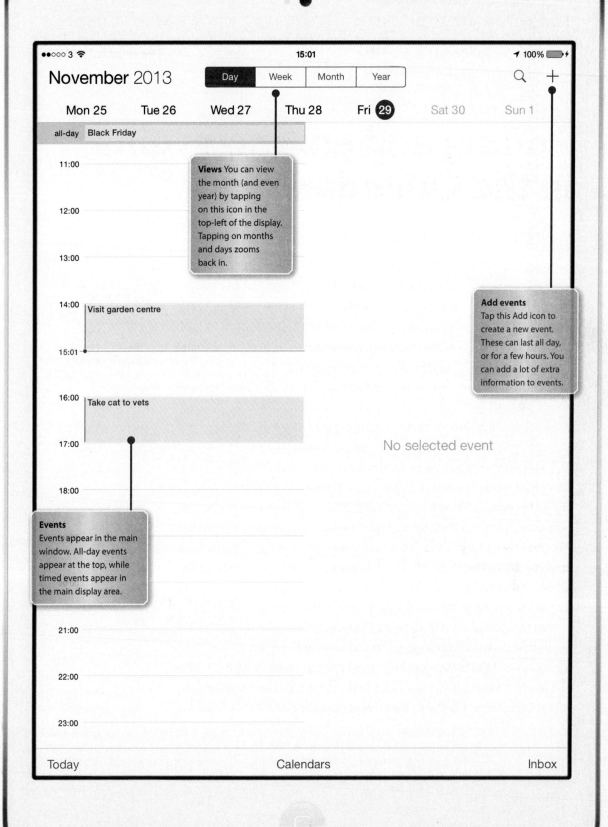

November 2013

| Day | Week | Month | Year |

| Mon 25 | Tue 26 | Wed 27 | Thu 28 | Fri 29 | Sat 30 | Sun 1 |

all-day Black Friday

11:00

12:00

13:00

Views You can view the month (and even year) by tapping on this icon in the top-left of the display. Tapping on months and days zooms back in.

14:00 Visit garden centre

15:01

16:00 Take cat to vets

17:00

18:00

Add events
Tap this Add icon to create a new event. These can last all day, or for a few hours. You can add a lot of extra information to events.

No selected event

Events
Events appear in the main window. All-day events appear at the top, while timed events appear in the main display area.

21:00

22:00

23:00

Today   Calendars   Inbox

STEP-BY-STEP GUIDE: **Managing your calendar**

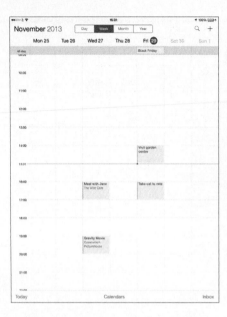

1 Different views You can switch between Day, Week, Month and Year view by tapping on the tabs at the top. You can scroll up and down through the hours of a day, or days in a month.

2 Add an event Tap the Add (+) icon at the top-right of the screen to create a new event. The keyboard will pop up and you can fill out the Title field with the name of your event.

3 Add details Tap inside the Location field to add the place where your event takes place. Note that these elements will be searchable, so it pays to type in something reasonably accurate.

4 Define a duration Tap the Starts and Ends fields to adjust the time of the event. Select Starts and use the barrel picker to define a time, and do the same for Ends. Tap outside the picker to set it.

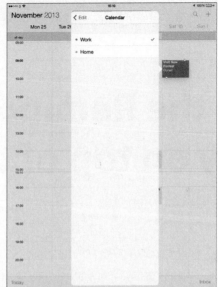

5 Set an alert Tap Alert to set an event alert time. You can pick from a set of predefined times. The alert appears as a notification at the set time. You can use Second Alert to add dual reminders.

6 Pick a calendar If the event you're adding isn't meant to be part of your default calendar, tap Calendar and select a different one. Multiple calendars can make it easier to manage a hectic life.

Automate

There's not much point in manually adding a recurring event to your calendar over and over again: that's because the Calendar app lets you automate the process by way of its Repeat menu item. Tap this to bring up the Repeat Event pop-up. Here you can define an event to repeat daily, weekly, fortnightly, monthly or annually.

7 Add notes Should your event need some more information use the Notes section. Notes are also searchable, so this is a good place to add memorable word associations.

8 Edit events Most event details can be edited. In day and list views, tap a selected event and Edit to change the details. In week and month views, tap a selected event and then the Edit button.

Using the Reminders app to stay on top of things

Never forget a thing with the Reminders app on your iPad

USING YOUR iPAD FOR REMINDERS AND TO-DO lists is a great idea. You're likely to have your iPad with you at all times so it just makes sense.

The rather aptly named Reminders app is here to help you with all your to-do lists. The Reminders app has some neat touches.

Integration with Siri is just one of the great features of Reminders. It takes merely a few seconds to set up a new reminder using just a push of the Home button and your voice.

Additionally, you can use GPS to activate reminders when you leave or arrive at certain places. So, for example, your iPad could remind you to pick up some milk on the way home as you leave work.

Naturally, you can set your own time-sensitive reminders, too, and if you have a lot of reminders you can easily search through them.

Reminders can be sorted in a list or by date and you can see a calendar view of all your reminders a month at a time.

If you're using the iCloud service all your reminders can be synched across devices. If you set a reminder on your iPad it will show on your iPhone and vice versa . If you're cursed with the forgetful gene, have no fear, the Reminders app is here. You'll never forget your wedding anniversary again. Here we show you how to use it.

KIT LIST:
- iPad
- iCloud account
- Internet connection

Time required: 15 mins
Difficulty: Beginner

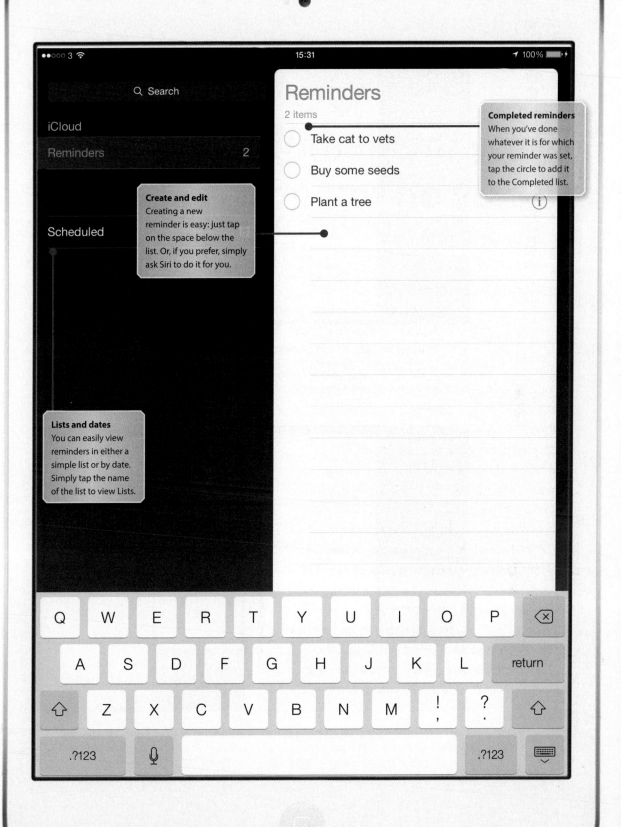

●●○○○ 3 🤖　　　　　　　　　　15:31　　　　　　　　🧭 100% 🔋⚡

Q Search

iCloud

Reminders　　　　　　　　　2

Scheduled

Reminders

2 items

◯ Take cat to vets

◯ Buy some seeds

◯ Plant a tree　　　　　　　　　　　　ⓘ

Completed reminders
When you've done whatever it is for which your reminder was set, tap the circle to add it to the Completed list.

Create and edit
Creating a new reminder is easy: just tap on the space below the list. Or, if you prefer, simply ask Siri to do it for you.

Lists and dates
You can easily view reminders in either a simple list or by date. Simply tap the name of the list to view Lists.

Q W E R T Y U I O P ⌫

A S D F G H J K L return

⇧ Z X C V B N M ! ? ⇧
　　　　　　　　　　　　　　, .

.?123 🎤 　　　　　　.?123 ⌨

STEP-BY-STEP GUIDE: Setting up Reminders

1 Reminders app Open the Reminders app to add a to-do item to your list. Here you'll see all your reminders and, if you're using iCloud, the account name used to synchronise reminders.

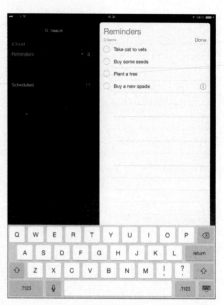

2 New reminder Tap on an empty line to create a reminder and the standard keyboard pops up. Type the reminder and tap Return. To edit it further simply tap on the reminder again.

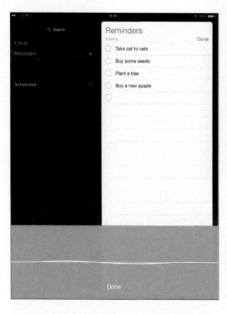

3 Dictate reminder If you don't want to type your reminder, you don't have to. Tap on the microphone icon next to the spacebar and simply speak your reminder. Tap Done to enter it.

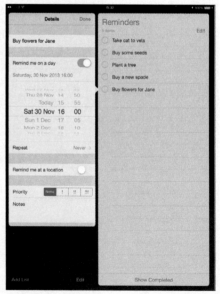

4 Remind me on a day To change the details about a reminder simply tap on it and tap on the Info ('i') icon. Tap 'Remind Me On A Day' to set a day when you want the iPad to alert you.

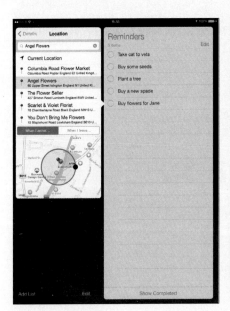

5 Location-based reminders You can
have a reminder pop up when you leave or arrive
somewhere. The iPad uses GPS to track you, and
when you're at the right spot it sends an alert.

6 See your month You can see all your
reminders in the month by tapping the Scheduled
item in the sidebar. This screen lists all your
reminders using the 'Remind Me On A Day' setting.

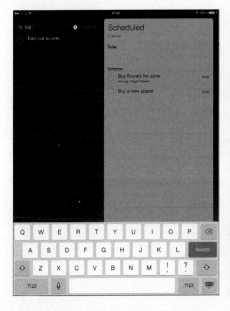

7 Search reminders If you can't see the
reminder you're after, use search. Tap on the search
field in the top-left and enter the item for which
you are looking.

8 Completed tasks Once you've comp[leted]
a tasks, you just tick it off by tapping the circl[e next]
to it. The task will be removed from the list, b[ut you]
can view it again by tapping Show Complete[d.]

Getting the most from your iPad's Music app

Get to grips with the music app on your iPad Air

THE MUSIC APP ON THE iPAD REPLACES THE iPOD app that was on some older iPads and iPhones. As you might expect the Music app is where you'll find all your audio files, including your iTunes songs, albums and playlists, plus any podcasts and audiobooks.

Although the name of the app has changed, the functionality hasn't altered all that much. If you've used the iPod app on a previous iOS device, you'll probably not notice the changes – they're that subtle in implementation.

One thing that has stayed the same is the flexibility of the app, although it remains easy to use. Getting to your favourite music is easy with options to create your own playlists on the iPad or have the Music app create some for you with Genius Playlists. With album artwork you can use the coverflow view to swipe through your albums by cover.

As well as helping you manage all the music you own, there's also a quick link to the iTunes Store to let you get your hands on even more. And if you have iTunes Match you can stream and download all the tracks from all your iTunes collections.

So, whether you want to hear the same song over and over again, or shuffle your songs to add a bit of variety, or just have Genius go to work and create some creative playlists for those long journeys to and from work or in the gym, this tutorial will help you get to grips with the app.

KIT LIST:
- iPad
- Apple ID
- Music and podcasts

Time required: 5 mins
Difficulty: Beginner

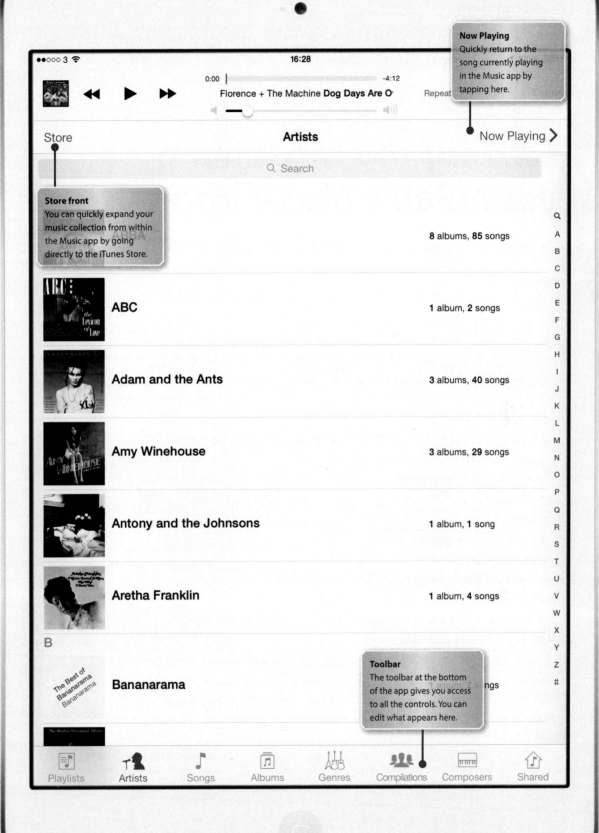

●●○○○ 3 📶 16:28

0:00   -4:12

◀◀ ▶ ▶▶   Florence + The Machine **Dog Days Are O'**   Repeat

Now Playing
Quickly return to the song currently playing in the Music app by tapping here.

Store   **Artists**   Now Playing ❯

Q Search

Store front
You can quickly expand your music collection from within the Music app by going directly to the iTunes Store.

8 albums, **85** songs

ABC   1 album, **2** songs

Adam and the Ants   3 albums, **40** songs

Amy Winehouse   3 albums, **29** songs

Antony and the Johnsons   1 album, **1** song

Aretha Franklin   1 album, **4** songs

B

Bananarama

Toolbar
The toolbar at the bottom of the app gives you access to all the controls. You can edit what appears here.

Q A B C D E F G H I J K L M N O P Q R S T U V W X Y Z #

Playlists   Artists   Songs   Albums   Genres   Compilations   Composers   Shared

STEP-BY-STEP GUIDE: Using the Music app

1 Artists By default you will see all music organised by artist. Scroll up and down to view your music and tap an artist name to view albums and tracks by that artist.

2 Search songs Tap on Songs to see all your music in alphabetical order. Tap Shuffle to listen to all your songs at random. Search for a specific song or simply swipe up and down.

3 Tap to play Tap on a track to start playing it through the iPad's speakers. The song will appear at the top next to the music controls. While it is playing you can view other tracks in the Music app.

4 Create playlists You can create playlists of your favourite tracks for easy access. Tap on Playlists, New Playlist. Enter a name and tap Save, then choose songs using the Add ("+") button.

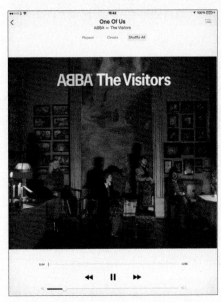

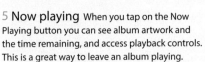

Music Genius

A neat way to get a quick playlist is to pick a song you like and tap Create, Genius Playlist. The Music app will pick a bunch of similar tracks to play.

5 Now playing When you tap on the Now Playing button you can see album artwork and the time remaining, and access playback controls. This is a great way to leave an album playing.

6 Double-tap When in the Now Playing view you can double-tap on the artwork image to get a full track listing. Just tap on another track in the album to quickly switch to it.

7 Music store Adding music to your collection is easier than ever. Simply tap on Store and you'll be taken directly to the iTunes Store. You can buy the latest songs and classics from here.

8 Music wherever Audio will continue to play when you press the Home button and move to other apps. You can use Control Centre to access controls (swipe up from the bottom of the screen).

Listen to all your music using iTunes Match

Stream every song you have in any iTunes with iTunes Match

ONE OF THE BIGGEST TECH TRENDS OF THE PAST few years is the shift to cloud computing, where you save and then access data on a remote server rather than on your own machine.

Naturally, Apple has put this to excellent use in iTunes, allowing users to store their entire music library 'in the cloud' and access it from any device without using up memory. Apple's service, called iTunes Match, scans your music library and either matches the track with a high-quality version from the iTunes Store or, if it doesn't have the track in its database, uploads your version to the cloud. Once complete, you can stream your tracks from any device (providing you have an active internet connection), without having to download them to that device.

If you do want a hard copy of a song on one of your machines, iTunes Match also lets you download it from the cloud free of charge. The best part: you can store up to 25,000 tracks, transforming your humble iPad into a serious music archive. What's more, you can access your songs from up to 10 iTunes-enabled devices.

Unsurprisingly, the service doesn't come for free – it will set you back £21.99 a year. However, as our tutorial will demonstrate, iTunes Match is easy to set up and use, and very versatile.

KIT LIST:

- **iTunes Match**
- **iPad**
- **Music tracks**

Time required: 5 mins
Difficulty: Beginner

▶

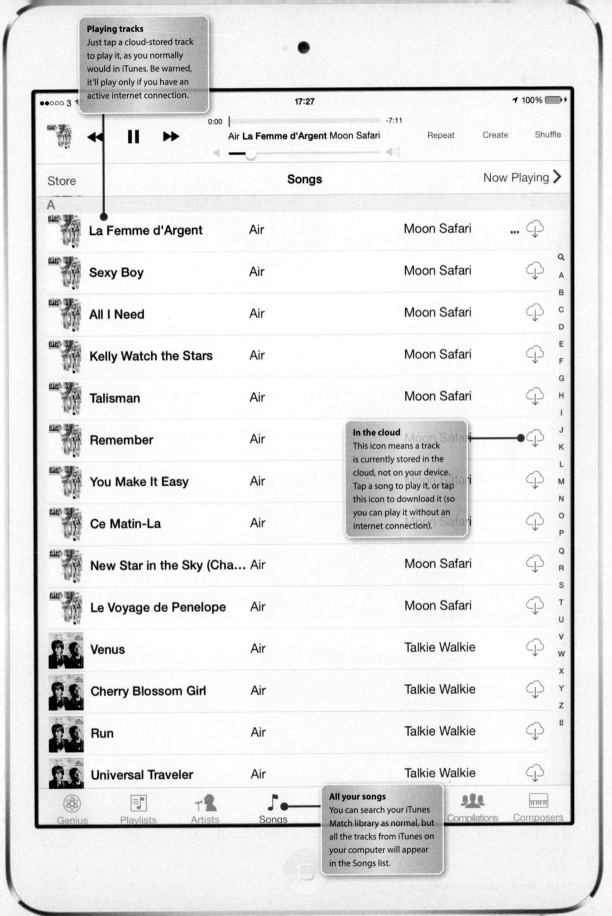

Playing tracks
Just tap a cloud-stored track to play it, as you normally would in iTunes. Be warned, it'll play only if you have an active internet connection.

17:27

100%

0:00 | ⏸ | -7:11

Air **La Femme d'Argent** Moon Safari

Repeat   Create   Shuffle

Store   **Songs**   Now Playing ❯

A

La Femme d'Argent   Air   Moon Safari   ...

Sexy Boy   Air   Moon Safari

All I Need   Air   Moon Safari

Kelly Watch the Stars   Air   Moon Safari

Talisman   Air   Moon Safari

Remember   Air   Moon Safari

In the cloud
This icon means a track is currently stored in the cloud, not on your device. Tap a song to play it, or tap this icon to download it (so you can play it without an internet connection).

You Make It Easy   Air   Moon Safari

Ce Matin-La   Air   Moon Safari

New Star in the Sky (Cha... Air   Moon Safari

Le Voyage de Penelope   Air   Moon Safari

Venus   Air   Talkie Walkie

Cherry Blossom Girl   Air   Talkie Walkie

Run   Air   Talkie Walkie

Universal Traveler   Air   Talkie Walkie

Q A B C D E F G H I J K L M N O P Q R S T U V W X Y Z #

Genius   Playlists   Artists   Songs   Compilations   Composers

All your songs
You can search your iTunes Match library as normal, but all the tracks from iTunes on your computer will appear in the Songs list.

1 Getting started First things first, you need to sign up to the Match service. Open iTunes on your Mac or PC desktop, click Store and choose 'Turn On iTunes Match'.

2 Matching tracks Follow the prompts and iTunes Match will automatically cycle through your music library, either matching tracks with those in its database or uploading any it doesn't recognise to your cloud.

3 Access tracks To listen to your library from your iPad, open Settings and then tap the Music tab in the lefthand menu. Toggle the iTunes Match switch to On. Hey presto, you're good to go.

4 Use cellular data Streaming music can quickly eat up a lot of your data contract. If you have an iPad with Cellular you might want to disable the 'Use Cellular Data' switch.

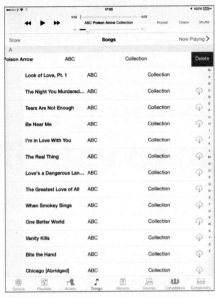

5 Downloading Should you want to download a track on to your device so you can listen to it without an internet connection just tap the cloud icon to the right of a track.

6 Deleting tracks If you find your device filling up and want to remove a song from your library and send it back to the cloud, just swipe over a track to the left to bring up a Delete tab.

Multiple devices

You can use iTunes Match on up to 10 devices per account. To link a device, make sure your signed in with your Apple ID. If it's an iOS device, go to Settings > Music > iTunes Match; if it's a computer just hit the iTunes Match tab in your iTunes menu panel.

7 Hiding cloud tracks If you'd rather your iPad displays only tracks that you currently have stored on your device, go back to Settings, bring up the Music tab and toggle off 'Show All Music'.

8 Resynching To resync your cloud library when you buy new music via your desktop iTunes hub, just bring up Settings, tap on the Store tab and toggle on Automatic downloads.

Downloading books and apps on to your iPad Air

Grab the best apps and books for your iPad Air

ONE OF THE THINGS THAT MAKES THE iPAD AIR experience so fantastic is the range of apps available for it. From the mundane productivity apps that help you work more efficiently to the fun stuff such as games, the iPad Air has more than enough to keep anybody entertained. The App Store is a major success story for Apple and app developers.

It's not just apps that Apple has turned its hand to either; books are now a major part of the iPad Air world. The fantastically sharp Retina display on the iPad Air means it's great for reading on the go. You can pack hundreds of books into your tablet and take them anywhere. Or, simply add to your collection from wherever you are in the world – no more hardback books to fit into your suitcase.

The App Store and iBookstore are, as you might expect from Apple, beautifully designed. Getting content from either of them is supremely simple. All that stands between you and millions of books and apps is a few taps on an iPad's screen.

Being able to get apps that enhance your iPad Air or books to keep you entertained, wherever you are and at any time, day or night, is amazing. There are restrictions that stop you from downloading larger apps over a mobile connection, so you may need to be on a wireless network for some.

Let's discover how to download apps on to your iPad Air.

KIT LIST:
- IPad
- Apple ID
- Internet connection

Time required: 5 mins
Difficulty: Beginner

▶

All Categories | Kids | Games | More | ☰ | 🔍 shazam ⊗

ANIMATION APPS

Plan Your WINTER BREAK

Best New Apps

Paper by FiftyThree	Radioline for iPad	MindNode	Spideo Movies	The Who Tommy	Fun Town for Kids - Creativ...	Framely
Productivity	Music	Productivity	Entertainment	Music	Education	Social Ne
FREE	FREE	£6.99	FREE	FREE	£0.69	FREE

App of the Week

INTERNATIONAL
FEDERATION
Philippine Typhoon Relief Donate Here

GAMES

ki
App

Best New Games

See All >

Icycle: On Thin Ice	The Inner World	FIFA 14 by EA SPORTS	Stampede Run HD	BADLAND	Adventure Town	Spiral Ep Free
Games	Games	Games	Games	Games	Games	Games
£0.69	£1.99	FREE	£0.69	£2.49	FREE	FREE

Essentials
APP COLLECTIONS

GAME COLLECTIONS

BAND IN YOUR HAND

Ser

STEP-BY-STEP GUIDE: Downloading books and apps

1 App Store To get started buying and downloading all the very best and latest apps, simply tap on the App Store icon on the Home screen of your iPad Air.

2 Store front The first time you open the App Store it will prompt you to download iBooks. You can also find a New link at the bottom that offers suggestions of apps you could download.

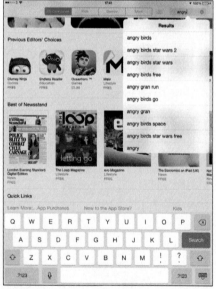

3 Get iBooks iBooks isn't one of the default iPad apps. You have to download iBooks from the App Store to buy books for your phone. Tap on iBooks, 'Free and Install' to get the app.

4 Find an app Tap on Search to find the exact app you're after. Type in its name and automatic suggestions will pop up. Tap on Search again if the App Store failed to find your app.

5 Buy your app Once you've found an app you want, all you have to do to get it is tap on the price, or Free if it's a free app, and then simply tap Install to get it on your device.

6 Empty shelves When you open iBooks for the first time your library is empty. To start downloading books, tap on Store at the top-right to flip the screen and open the iBook Store.

Large print

One of the advantages of reading books on the iPad Air is you can edit the layout to suit your taste. Tap the font icon (ᴀA) to make the print bigger or smaller, or on the magnifying glass to search its pages.

7 iBooks Store As with the App Store, there are suggestions and charts. Simply tap on a book, then the price and, finally, Buy Book. The download will begin immediately.

8 Full library Any books you buy will automatically be added to your library. To start reading just tap on a cover. To remove a book tap on Edit, then the book, then Delete.

Read the latest digital magazines with Newsstand

Subscribe to your favourite magazines right from your iPad

IN THE DAYS BEFORE THE INTERNET, SUBSCRIBING to a magazine was a great way to keep up to date with the latest news about your favourite subjects. But the web has changed this for many, and the lure of instant information has been difficult to resist.

How can you cope with the deluge of data available in a web browser? It's possible to spend all day reading garbage online and not learn a thing. Many people long to read in-depth articles, books (such as this one), and classic magazines such as *Macworld* or *iPad & iPhone User* in a new digital form.

Newsstand is designed to bridge the gap between the print and online publishing worlds. It combines the richness of published material with a highly convenient way of accessing that information wherever you happen to be, all from the comfort of your iPad (the best part is that you can also get the same content for your iPhone and iPod touch via the same app).

You can choose to buy individual issues or subscribe for a set period of time. When you select the latter, new issues will automatically appear in your Newsstand, without you even having to get up and pick up the mail.

Newsstand isn't an exclusive feature of the iPad Air. In fact, it can be used on any iOS device, even the earlier iPads, but the sheer quality of the iPad Air's screen makes reading magazines and newspapers that much more of a pleasant experience – it feels as though you're looking at glossy print.

So let's discover how to download and read magazines on the iPad.

KIT LIST:
- iPad
- Internet connection
- iTunes account

Time required: 5 mins
Difficulty: Beginner

Preview
Tap Options and Preview to view a magazine before you buy it. Swipe left and right to navigate through the pages.

Buy magazine
Tap the price of a magazine to buy it and read it directly on your iPad.

OVER 40% SAVING

SUBSCRIBE FOR AS LITTLE AS £1.42/$2.28 PER ISSUE

THE APPLE EXPERTS
Macworld
MAC / iPHONE / iPAD

TAP HERE TO VIEW OUR LATEST SUBSCRIPTION OFFERS

£2.49

Options

Christmas 2013

In the latest issue of Macworld we explain how to get more from OS X Mavericks, with 83 expert tips. There's also our complete guide to buying an iPad, Christmas wishlist, plus a bumper reviews section that includes the 13- and 15in MacBook Pro with Retina display, iPad Air, iPad mini with Retina display, OS X Mavericks, and iWork and iLife for both Mac and iOS. Don't miss out!

Read back issues
Swipe left and right across these magazine covers to see back issues.

NEW iPad AIR REVIEWED
THE WORLD'S BEST-SELLING APPLE MAGAZINE
Macworld
OS X MAVERICKS 83 EXPERT TIPS
Get more from Apple's new operating system PLUS in-depth review
NEW Retina MacBook Pro
Apple's new 13- & 15-inch laptops tested, now from £1,099
REVIEWED: iWORK & iLIFE FOR MAC & iOS
COMPLETE GUIDE TO BUYING AN iPAD

EXCLUSIVE: NEW iPADS LAUNCHED
Macworld
NEW iMACS
REVIEWED: Apple's new iMacs fully tested
NEW SUPER-FAST PROCESSOR FROM £1,149
OS 7 TIPS
PC USER'S GUIDE TO MAC
iPHONE PHOTO SHOOTOUT

COMPLETE GUIDE
Macworld
FULL REVIEWS
iPhone 5S & iPhone 5C
New Apple iPhone buying advice
Full UK network pricing information
TOP 40 MAC APPS
Micro SLRs FROM £399

Purchased   Specials   2013   2012   2011   2010

100s of tips inside!

The complete guide to the **iPad 4**
The ultimate guide to Apple's latest iPad
Available to buy within this app

The complete guide to the iPad 4
100s inside!

1 The Newsstand Find the Newsstand icon; this is the folder in which all your magazines and newspapers are stored. Tap on it to reveal any publications that are available to read.

2 The Store If this is the first time you've opened Newsstand it should be empty, so tap on the Store button. This launches the App Store (of which the Newsstand's store is a subset).

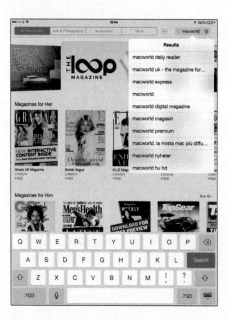

3 Search field You can either browse magazines from the Newsstand, or use the search field in the top-right to search for your favourite magazines.

4 Getting Results If you search for a popular magazine you might find international results. Tap the version you are interested in to see more details (we are looking for *Macworld UK*).

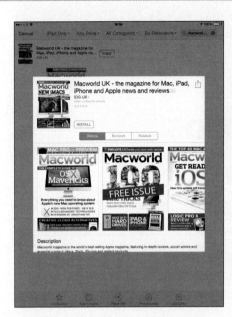

5 Preview You can tap on Details in the list to see a description of what you're about to buy. Most magazines are free to download, but you then have to pay for each edition you want to read.

6 Download Select your magazine and it'll download to your iPad. Most magazines will send you push notifications when a new edition is available, saving you from checking.

Reordering

Magazines are organised in the Newsstand in the order in which they were purchased, with the latest ones appearing on the left. This can be changed, just like with regular apps: tap and hold on one of them and they all start to jiggle, then drag and drop them into the order that works best for you.

7 Issue selection You get to look through all the editions available for your magazine. You can buy one by tapping the price above the cover. It will download to your magazine.

8 Enjoy You can preview a magazine by tapping on Options, Preview. This is a great way to check out what you're buying. When you buy the magazine the full version will be downloaded.

Take amazing photos with the Camera app

Capture great photographs and save them direct to your iPad Air

THE iPAD AIR HAS AN AMAZING SET OF CAMERAS, much better than those found on the iPad 2, which appeared to be the same type as the one found on the iPod touch.

However, such poor images wouldn't have done the iPad Air's amazing screen justice, so Apple beefed up the camera and it's now capable of taking 5Mp shots with the iSight camera (the one on the back of the iPad) and 1.2Mp shots with the front-facing FaceTime camera. It can also record video in high-definition (1080p), just like the iPhone.

In addition to this vastly superior camera, Apple has updated the Camera app, making it much easier to take photos with this rather bulky device when compared with a regular camera. Its camera may be of a lesser quality than your point-and-shoot, but you won't struggle to take pictures with your iPad.

The Camera app enables you to snap photographs and shoot video using both the rear-facing (iSight) and front-facing (FaceTime) cameras. The Camera app keeps things simple, but there are a few options available to you. You can record still photos, square photos and video footage, and choose between regular and HDR (high dynamic range) photographs.

This tutorial will guide you through the Camera app's various options. Follow this guide and you'll be capturing amazing photographs in no time.

KIT LIST:
- **iPad**
- **Something to shoot**
- **The urge to shoot it**

Time required: 5 mins
Difficulty: Beginner

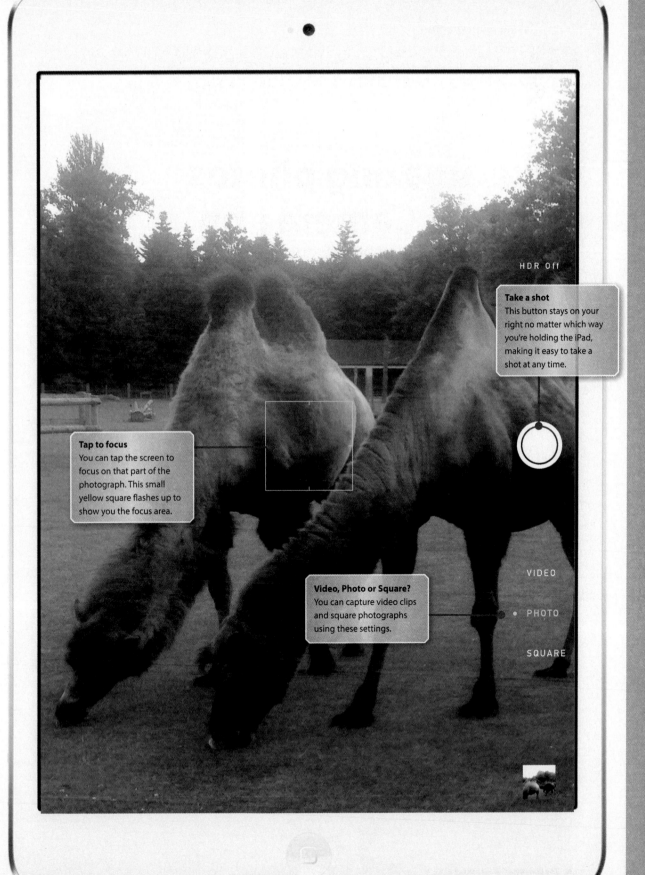

HDR Off

Take a shot
This button stays on your right no matter which way you're holding the iPad, making it easy to take a shot at any time.

Tap to focus
You can tap the screen to focus on that part of the photograph. This small yellow square flashes up to show you the focus area.

VIDEO

Video, Photo or Square?
You can capture video clips and square photographs using these settings.

PHOTO

SQUARE

STEP-BY-STEP GUIDE: Using the Camera app

1 To the right Launch the Camera app and you'll see what's in the lens on the screen. The controls are always on the right, no matter which way around you hold the iPad.

2 Focus Tap on the star of your shot to focus on that area. A small yellow square will appear indicating where the current focus is. You can change this as many times as you want.

3 HDR On You can take a much higher shot by tapping the HDR Off button to turn on HDR. This will take higher-quality shots, although they take up more space on the iPad.

4 Take a shot When you're ready, take a shot by pressing the white shutter button. If you prefer, you can also use the physical volume up button to take your photo.

5 **Video** Slide your finger down the screen to turn the iPad into a camcorder. You can see Video, Photo and Square modes on the right. When you hit the record button, you'll see a timer, too.

6 **Camera Roll** To view the photos you've taken, tap on the Camera Roll button (bottom-right). This shows you the last shot you took. Swipe to the left to see others, one at a time.

Photos app

After you've finished using the Camera you can view your photos in the Photos app. This is a separate app to the Camera, and organises your photo collection by Years (above), Collections, Moments and individual Photos.

7 **Edit** You can edit your photos within Camera Roll. Press the Edit button to bring up a set of options such as Rotate, Enhance, Filters, Red-Eye and Crop. Tap an option then Apply and Save.

8 **Share your photos** You can share your shots in various ways. Tap on the Camera Roll, then the Share icon (bottom-left). Choose Mail, Message or another way to share your photograph.

Using the iPad Air to edit photographs

Edit photos on your iPad Air to make them even better

NOW THAT YOU'VE TAKEN YOUR PICTURES AND, if you're using iCloud, sent them to your Photo Stream, you might just want to leave them there. However, no matter how good a camera you possess, some judicious image editing can always help to improve the final result.

You might want to make the colours and contrast stand out, and sometimes a small crop is all that's needed to make a good picture a fantastic one. If you've taken a photo of friends and they all have the dreaded red-eye, you'll want to get rid of that.

Luckily, thanks to the power of the dual-core A7 chip inside the iPad Air, your tablet is a powerful image-editing tool. The Retina display also helps you to be more accurate, thanks to the fantastic detail it provides.

The iPad Air itself lets you make your pictures look better with a single tap. It can also help you with some of the usual pitfalls of photography. If you take a shot of people with the flash, sometimes they'll have red-eye. To help you make your subjects look a little less like they've been possessed by the devil, you can quickly and simply remove the red-eye.

There's also a crop tool that allows you to cut out the best bit of a photo and reframe your shot for a better result. And you can add a range of effects to your photos with the tap of a button.

If you want to take image editing further you can download any number of apps to help you do more with your pictures, too.

KIT LIST:
- iPad
- Photos

Time required: 10 mins
Difficulty: Beginner

STEP-BY-STEP GUIDE: Editing photos on your iPad Air

1 Start editing Go to your images in the Photos app, then tap on the one you'd like to edit. Simply tap on Edit to bring up the iPad's editing options.

2 Editing tools The iPad Air's editing tools are displayed across the bottom of the screen. You can rotate, enhance or crop your image, and remove red-eye. Simply tap on one to get started.

3 Rotate your pictures If you've taken a picture at a funny angle, or you want to have some fun with a picture, you can rotate it. Tap on Rotate at the bottom-left to spin your image.

4 Enhance your images The iPad has a simple Enhance mode that automatically improves the colour and contrast of your images. Tap Enhance to instantly improve the colour of a photo.

5 Fix red-eye If the image has been taken with a flash (on the iPhone or other camera), it can end up with nasty red-eye ruining your shot. Tap on the red-eye button and then on the 'infected' eye.

6 Tap the eye Tap each of the eyes to remove the red circle. When done, tap on Apply to save your changes. It might not always work perfectly, but it's generally effective.

App Store

The built-in tools for editing photos are pretty good, but they are very basic. You can get more advanced image-editing tools from the App Store. Many of these are free or fairly cheap.

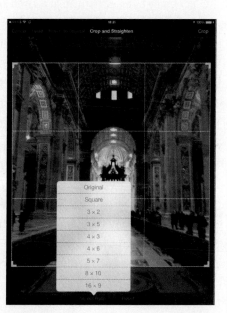

7 Add an effect Tap on Filters to add an effect to an image. There is a range of filters, such as Chrome and Transfer. Tap around to see what effect they have. If you like an effect tap Apply.

8 Crop images To crop images tap on the Crop tool, then drag in the corners of the grid to suit. You can also tap Aspect Ratio to crop an image to a set size. Tap Crop when you're done.

Using iPhoto to make photographs look amazing

Discover how to use the iPhoto app and create great-looking shots

AS ANY PHOTOGRAPHER WORTH THEIR SALT WILL tell you, there's much more to taking a great picture than simply pointing your camera at something and releasing the shutter. Often, it's what you do after the event that makes an image memorable.

Every shot you see in a magazine or newspaper has generally been enhanced in a variety of ways to make it as eye-catching as possible. Crooked images can be straightened, dull colours can be enhanced, strong focal points can be cropped in on, filters can be applied for dramatic effect – the list goes on.

With Apple's supremely easy-to-use iPhoto editing suite finally making its way to the iPad, you can now harness just this sort of magic from your tablet. The iOS version of the popular Mac program has survived the transition to iPad with almost all of its features intact, and a handful of new ones thrown in. What's more, the new touchscreen functionality makes it more intuitive and accessible than ever before.

With a little practice you'll be able to work on your images with a number of clearly defined tools, before cataloguing them, tagging them and sharing them with friends via email or social networks. And with the iPad Air's crystal clear Retina screen and added processing oomph, they'll look better than ever to boot. Read on for our step-by-step guide.

KIT LIST:
- iPad
- iPhoto app
- Some photos

Time required: 20 mins
Difficulty: Intermediate

Undo
If you're not happy with one of the changes you've made, just tap this arrow to go back a step.

Show original
Hitting this tab will remove all the changes you've made to an image and revert to the original shot. Just swipe this slider to the right.

Look at the loupe
Touch the screen with two fingers and twist to bring up the magnifying glass tool, allowing you to zoom in on your shot.

Editing tools
You'll find all your filters, brushes, effects and cropping tools here. A blue marker above a tab means you've already used it in your image.

Flagged up
Tap the flag button and your image will be filed in the Flagged folder for future reference. Tap it again to remove the flag.

STEP-BY-STEP GUIDE: Using iPhoto

1 Organisation iPhoto organises your images by Photos, Albums and Projects. Pictures you take using the iPad's camera will appear in Photos and a Camera Roll area at the top of Albums. Start by tapping on Albums and picking a collection.

2 Select an image Tap on any image and a large preview will appear. You can view other photos from the album using the Thumbnail Grid at the bottom (you can remove this by tapping the Thumbnail Grid icon in the top left).

3 Straighten up Our wonky post shows that this shot is clearly off-centre. To correct it, hit the Crop button bottom left and drag the Straighten wheel at the bottom. Tap Crop again to finish.

4 Enhancing colours Hit Auto-Enhance (the magic wand icon) to quickly improve an image. Or tap Exposure and drag the Brightness and Contrast buttons on the slider to manually adjust.

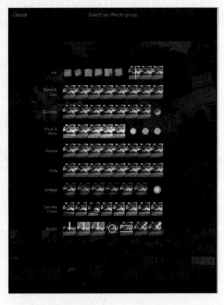

5 Do it yourself You can also manually adjust the colour settings. Tap colour and you will find four sliders: Saturation, Blue Skies, Greenery and Warmth. Drag these left or right to adjust the colour levels of a photograph.

6 Add a filter Reckon your image might look better in black and white? No problem – just bring up the Effects menu in the toolbar. There are a range of filters to choose from; select one then swipe on the image to adjust the effect.

Built-in help

iPhoto offers one of the best help features we've seen in a piece of Apple software. Just hit the 'question mark' tab on the top menu bar and a comprehensive overlay of labels explaining what every button does will appear on the screen. Tap it one more time to toggle back to the normal view.

7 Brush up an image You can paint effects on to your photo using Brushes. Here we've chosen Saturate and drawn on the sky to create a more vibrant effect.

8 Title and share Once you've finished tweaking your image you can label it for future reference by tapping on 'Add a caption' at the top of the screen. Finally, tap Share.

Viewing photos as Years, Collections and Moments

View your photographs using the iOS 7 Photos app

WITH iOS 7 INCLUDED ON THE iPAD AIR COMES a whole new way of organising your photo collection.

Images are now grouped together by Years, Collections, Moments and Photos. In Years view the photos are tiny thumbnails and you can see all your photos taken over the years. The pictures are too small to enjoy in this mode, but thanks to the iPad's Retina display you can roughly determine the subject matter.

Tapping on an area of photos in the Years view takes you into Collections. These are groups of photographs based upon a certain time and place. Above each group of images will be the name of the place and rough date that they were taken.

Tap again to go to Moments – groups of pictures all taken at the same place and time. If you went on holiday to Paris, for example, the Collection would be the holiday and the moment would be the Eiffel tower, the Louvre, eating snails in a restaurant and so on.

You bounce back up from Photos to Moments, then Collections and finally back to Years using the corresponding icon in the top-left of the display. It may seem a bit of an overload at first, especially the Years view, but you quickly get used to zooming in and out of pictures.

Let's take a look at how photos are organised on the iPad.

KIT LIST:
- iPad
- Photos

Time required: 10 mins
Difficulty: Beginner

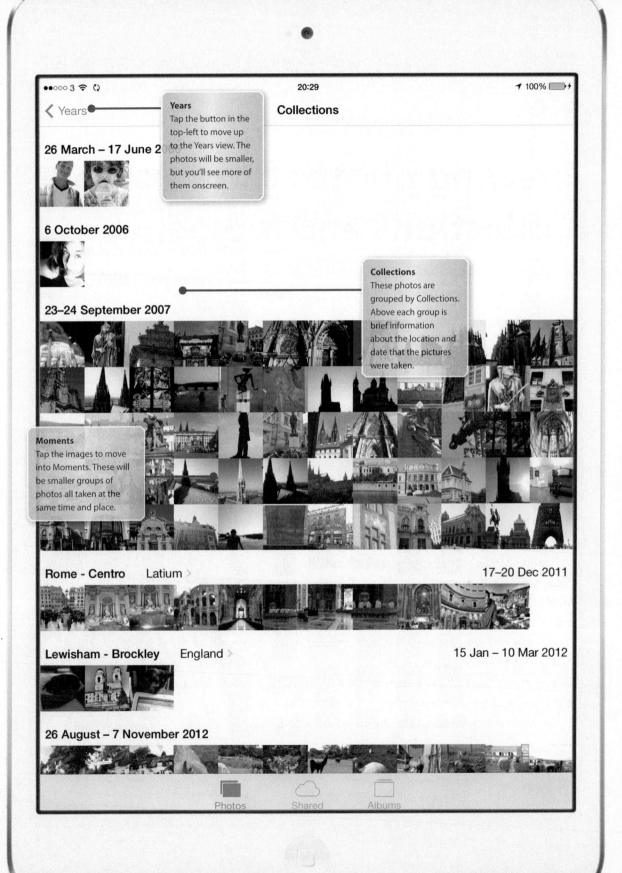

26 March – 17 June 2

Years
Tap the button in the top-left to move up to the Years view. The photos will be smaller, but you'll see more of them onscreen.

6 October 2006

Collections
These photos are grouped by Collections. Above each group is brief information about the location and date that the pictures were taken.

23–24 September 2007

Moments
Tap the images to move into Moments. These will be smaller groups of photos all taken at the same time and place.

Rome - Centro   Latium ›   17–20 Dec 2011

Lewisham - Brockley   England ›   15 Jan – 10 Mar 2012

26 August – 7 November 2012

Photos   Shared   Albums

STEP-BY-STEP GUIDE: Editing photos on your iPad

1 Years This top-level view shows all the photos as tiny thumbnails. This is a good overview of all your photos. Scroll up and down and tap on a group of photos to move to a Collection.

2 Collections In the Collections view you'll see larger thumbnails. Photos are now grouped by time and date. You can move up and down through these. Tap on a Collection to view a Moment.

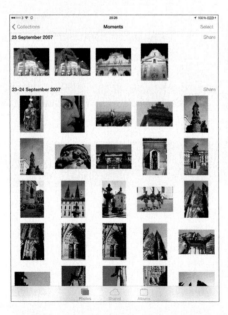

3 Moments In the Moments view you will see photos grouped closely together in a time and place. They should be large enough to see clearly. Tap on a photo to view it.

4 Each photo The individual photos are displayed one at a time onscreen. You can use pinch-to-zoom and slide left and right between photos.

5 Sharing Tap Moments (top-left) to zoom back up the Collections view. Now tap Shared in the bottom tab. Here you can see recently shared photos.

6 Set up a stream Tap Create New Stream and give your Stream a name (such as 'Family Photos'). Now enter the email address of a person with whom you'd like to share those photos.

Shared streams
It's easy to share photos as 'Streams' using iCloud. Tap Shared, then Add (top-left). Give your stream a name and tap Next. Enter a person's email address and tap Done. Tap on pictures to select them, then tap Done to share.

7 Creating albums Tap on photos you'd like to share, or tap the Select button next to a Moment. Then tap Done. You can repeat the process to add more photos later.

8 Sharing If your friend has an iPhone or iPad they will see the photos in their Shared tab. Now any photos you share with this Stream will appear on their iPad as well.

Taking and editing video directly on the iPad

Discover how to capture and edit video clips

WHILE THE iPAD AIRS'S CRYSTAL CLEAR RETINA display hogs all the headlines, Apple's spent a lot of time ensuring that the iPad is just as good at recording video as it is playing it. The new iSight camera is a quiet revolution for the tablet, offering a 5Mp lens and the ability to shoot 1080p video with auto stabilisation to smooth bumps and shakes.

KIT LIST:
- iPad
- Something to shoot

Time required: 5 mins
Difficulty: Beginner

That's a significant improvement over the iPad 2, which boasted a humble 0.7Mp lens capable of shooting only up to 720p. You'll really notice the difference, especially on that lovely Retina display.

The camera is an important part of the iPad's impressive feature set, making it a true jack-of-all-trades multimedia device. Spot something filmworthy going on? Pick up your iPad, bring up the camera app and hit record. Once your done, head over to iMovie and edit your footage into a proper movie, perhaps adding some music you've composed in GarageBand. Quickly upload it to YouTube in-app, and within 30 minutes of filming a video clip you could be an internet sensation.

It's all extremely easy to use. There are no calibrations to make, dials to twiddle or menus to navigate – just point at your subject and start shooting. There's even an idiotproof autofocus feature to ensure your film looks professional. And Apple makes it easy to trim your video, or you can edit it using a professional app such as iMovie. With a bit of practise you'll be turning around feature films in no time.

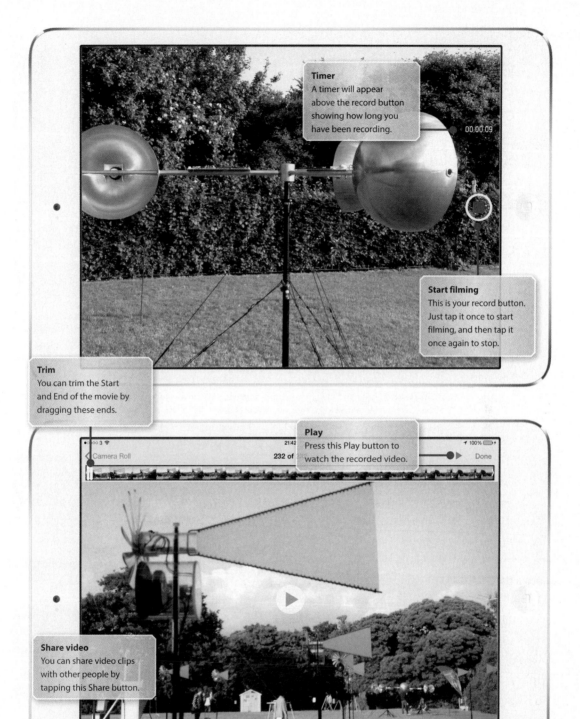

Timer
A timer will appear above the record button showing how long you have been recording.

00:00:09

Start filming
This is your record button. Just tap it once to start filming, and then tap it once again to stop.

Trim
You can trim the Start and End of the movie by dragging these ends.

Play
Press this Play button to watch the recorded video.

Share video
You can share video clips with other people by tapping this Share button.

Camera Roll   21:42   232 of   100%   Done

STEP-BY-STEP GUIDE: Recording video

1 Getting started First things first, there's not a separate app for video capture so don't go looking for one. Just tap on your iPad's Camera app to get started.

2 Hit record To begin filming you need to switch to video mode. Toggle the slider in the bottom-right of the screen to the camera icon. Then set up your shot and hit the red record button.

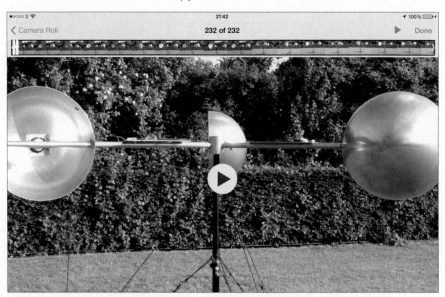

3 Keeping time As you're filming a timer will appear in the top-right corner of the screen. Bear in mind that video can take up a lot of storage space, so keep your videos short.

4 Video playback When you're done recording, tap the small square icon in the bottom-left corner to bring up your library. Then just tap on the play icon to watch it back.

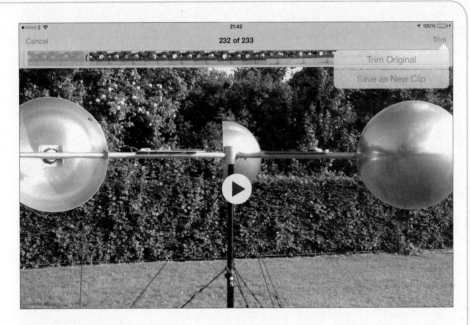

Trim Original

Save as New Clip

5 Trim bars You can trim the end of your videos to focus on the action. Just drag the Trim bars on the left and right of the Preview bar at the top to focus on the part of the video you want.

6 Save the video When you've selected the part of the video you want. Tap the Trim button in the top-right. Select Trim Original to remove the unwanted footage, or Save As New Clip.

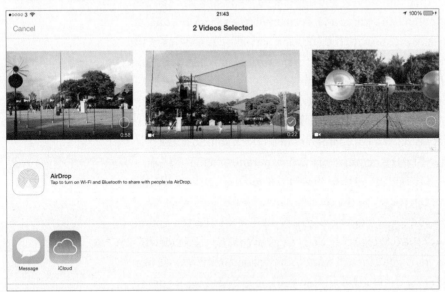

AirDrop
Tap to turn on Wi-Fi and Bluetooth to share with people via AirDrop.

Message   iCloud

7 Share with friends To immediately share the clip with a friend, upload it to YouTube or simply email it to yourself, just tap the Share icon in the bottom right.

8 Editing in iMovie To really make the most of your footage, it's worth picking the iMovie app (£2.99). Apple's acclaimed editing software lets you combine clips into a full movie.

Don't spin it

You can record video in either portrait or landscape mode. Landscape generally looks better on a television, but both are pretty good for showing off on the iPad. Don't switch from one to the other while filming, though. The display will orientate itself and you think everything is okay, but it'll be recording footage at a 90 degree angle. Be careful to stick to either one or the other.

Using Maps to find places and get directions

You can navigate your way around using the Maps application

IF YOU ARE FOREVER GETTING LOST THEN THE iPAD could prove to be a real lifesaver. It's great at knowing where you are, even if you aren't entirely sure. The powerful GPS inside the Wi-Fi + Cellular model combines with local mobile reception towers to give incredibly accurate positioning. Apple has built its own mapping service and app, called Maps, and you can use it to find local information, directions and even use it as a satnav in your car.

The app, used in conjunction with the Location Services capabilities of the iPad, makes it incredibly simple to find where you are, and provide directions for you to make it from A to B as quickly as possible.

You can map your journey by car, public transport or walking, and there are alternative routes for you to choose from, too. You can search around you for local businesses or, indeed, companies in any location. So if, for example, you need to find the nearest Post Office, garage or supermarket, you can use your iPad to find it and then have it tell you the quickest route.

Apple's Maps app can show you the standard map view of your route or, if you prefer, it'll show you the satellite view overhead. There's also the option to get a hybrid view of the two together. You can even see the street view if it's available, giving you a good idea of what your final destination looks like.

If you have an AirPrint-compatible printer, you can get hard copies of the map and, if the graphics get too much for you, it's possible to see your journey in list view so that it's just the instructions. Get mapping your routes on the iPad using the following tutorial.

KIT LIST:

- **iPad**
- **Internet connection**
- **Place to go**

Time required: 5 mins
Difficulty: Beginner

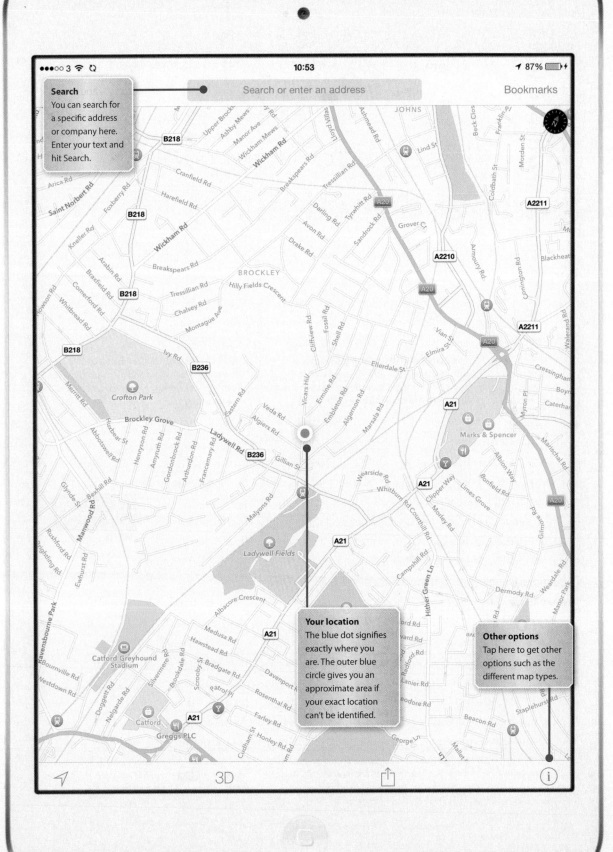

Search
You can search for a specific address or company here. Enter your text and hit Search.

Search or enter an address

Bookmarks

Your location
The blue dot signifies exactly where you are. The outer blue circle gives you an approximate area if your exact location can't be identified.

Other options
Tap here to get other options such as the different map types.

3D

STEP-BY-STEP GUIDE: Finding places and directions

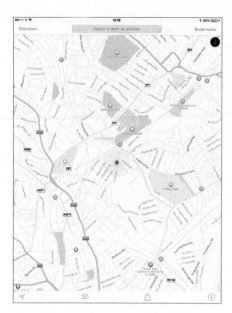

1 Map your route Open the Maps app and tap the Location arrow-shaped icon in the bottom-right corner. Your current location should be displayed as a pulsing blue circle.

2 Using the compass Tap the Location arrow-shaped icon again and Maps will show you which way you are facing. As you move around the map spins with you.

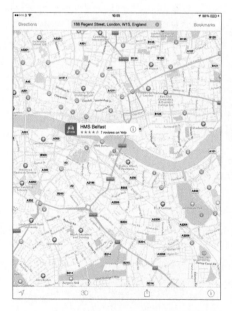

3 What's nearby? On the map you will see lots of small icons. These are local businesses or points of interest. Tap on one to see more details. If you tap on the blue car you will get directions.

4 More info Tap on the small Info icon ('i') to view more information about a place. You can see the address, phone number and website. There are often reviews and photos to look at, too.

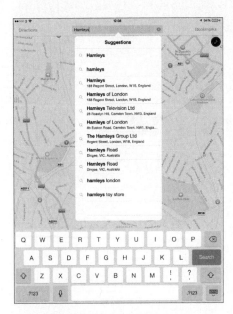

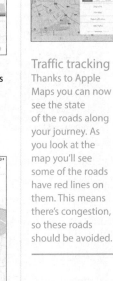

5 Find a place You can search for places using the Search box at the top. A list of suggestions will appear; tap on one to find that place. If you want to go there tap on Directions in the top right.

6 Route Maps will offer you a selection of routes to get to the place. You can stick with the default route, or tap on one of the fainter options to use that route instead.

Traffic tracking
Thanks to Apple Maps you can now see the state of the roads along your journey. As you look at the map you'll see some of the roads have red lines on them. This means there's congestion, so these roads should be avoided.

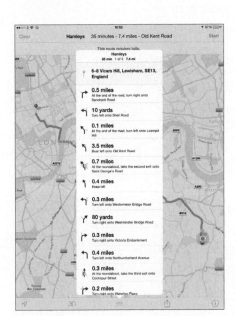

7 List of turns Tap on the List icon at the bottom to view a list of steps in your route. This can be handy to look at before you go. Tap on the Start button to begin navigating to the place.

8 Step by step Maps will now act like a satnav, guiding you to your location. You can tap Overview at any time to see the whole route, or End to stop the navigation.

Viewing a city from the air with Flyover

The Flyover mode in Maps enables you to view cities in 3D

THE MAPS APP ON THE iPAD AIR REPLACES Google's Street View with Flyover. This is a fantastic 3D effect that enables you to fly around photorealistic cities.

As you pan and zoom around cities, you can switch to Satellite mode and get an accurate photographic top-down view of a location. With Flyover it's also possible to rotate the view so you can see how buildings look from the side – it's almost like flying around a city.

Flyover is an incredibly impressive feature that can be found only on the iPad. Accessing the Flyover mode couldn't be easier: open Maps, switch to Satellite mode, zoom in and pan around. The technology behind it is pretty amazing: Apple has flown helicopters and planes around all major cities, taking photographs of buildings from all angles. It's then got designers to stitch those photographs on to 3D wireframe models of cities. The result is indistinguishable from real life.

Flyover may not be the most practical feature (unless you plan on flying around a city like Superman), but it is one of the best ways to show off the iPad's Retina Display.

In this tutorial we'll take a look at how to get the most out of Flyover.

KIT LIST:
- iPad
- Internet connection
- Flyover area

Time required: 5 mins
Difficulty: Beginner

Cities in 3D
Flyover shows major cities in photographic 3D. Use pinch and rotate gestures to fly around a cityscape.

Satellite view
Change to Satellite view by tapping this Info icon in the bottom right of the screen and choosing Satellite.

Flyover button
Press the Flyover button to rotate the angle of view by 45 degrees.

STEP-BY-STEP GUIDE: Using Flyover

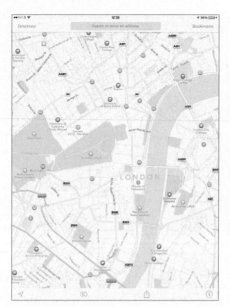

1 Open Maps Start by opening the Maps app and navigate to a major city. Not everywhere has Flyover so try London, Manchester or Birmingham in the UK.

2 Zoom Use the pinch-to-zoom gesture to get a nice close-up of some central part of a city. This will help show off Flyover in all its glory.

3 Tap Flyover Tap the Flyover button in the bottom left of the screen to rotate the Map into 3D. Building shapes will spring up out of the ground.

4 Satellite mode Flyover works best in Satellite mode. Tap the Info icon (the small 'i') in the bottom-right of Maps and tap on Satellite.

5 Rotate up and down You can adjust the Flyover angle by putting two fingers on the display and pushing up. This gesture also rotates the view.

6 Move around You can move around in Flyover view by putting a single finger on the screen and moving it around. It may take longer to load the map than usual.

Flyover with more details
You can use the Hybrid mode to view both the satellite imagery and the map information (roads names and so on). This is a great way to get a good overview of particular areas of a city.

7 Zoom in and out You zoom in and out by using the pinch-to-zoom gesture. It's possible to get close to the buildings and see their finer details.

8 Rotate You can get a good view of all sides of a building by placing two fingers on the screen and using the Rotate gesture (two fingers in a circle).

Using AirPlay and AirDrop to share files

Mirroring the iPad display to a large-screen TV is easy with AirPlay

THE iPAD IS A POWERFUL HANDHELD DEVICE that enables you to view, edit and play many of the files you'd normally see on a computer. You can take photographs, watch videos, play music and create business documents, all from the palm of your hand.

And although the iPad has a sharp Retina display and an immaculate speaker, there are times when you want to send its audio or video to a dedicated device. Apple has a technology called AirPlay that enables you to do just this: you can play music wirelessly from your iPad on an AirPlay speaker, or play video stored on your iPad on a television set using an Apple TV.

Into this powerful mix comes a new technology called AirDrop. AirDrop enables you to share files on your iPad with any other iOS device in the local vicinity. Simply enable AirDrop, pick a photo, web page or other document and tap Share. You can then send it straight to your friend's device. This is great for sharing photographs directly with other people.

AirPlay works via Wi-Fi and other AirPlay-compatible devices – typically an AirPlay speaker and Apple TV inside your house. AirDrop uses both Bluetooth and Wi-Fi, and requires you and your friend to be in the same location and connected to the same Wi-Fi network.

In this tutorial we'll look at how to use AirDrop and AirPlay to share files from your iPad.

KIT LIST:
- iPad
- Wi-Fi connection
- Apple TV

Time required: 15 mins
Difficulty: Intermediate

▶

Messages

Photos

Camera

Maps

Clock

Photo Booth

Calendar

Contacts

Notes

Reminders

Newsstand

Game Center

Settings

FaceTime

Control Centre
AirDrop and AirPlay are both set up in iOS 7's Control Centre. This can be accessed by dragging your finger up from the bottom of the display.

Bluetooth and Wireless
AirDrop requires both Bluetooth and Wireless to be turned on. It will automatically turn on both when activated (and leave them on).

AirDrop
Tap this button in Control Centre to activate AirDrop. You can share files with everybody in the local vicinity, or just people in your Contacts list.

AirDrop: Everyone

AirPlay

AirPlay
Tap this button to turn on AirPlay. You can share music with AirPlay-compatible speakers and photos and video with an Apple TV device.

STEP-BY-STEP GUIDE: Streaming photos & video

1 Activate AirDrop Open Control Centre by sliding your finger up from the bottom of the display. Tap AirDrop and choose either Everyone or Contacts Only. It's easier to share with Everyone.

2 Share a photo Open the Photos app and view a single picture. Tap the Share icon in the bottom left to view the sharing window. You'll see an AirDrop section just below the photo.

3 Tap to share If another person in the area turns on AirDrop on their iPad or iPhone they will appear in your AirDrop section. Tap their name to send the photo to them.

4 Accept the file The recipient will get a pop-up asking whether they want the file. If they click Accept the file goes straight into the same app on their device as on yours.

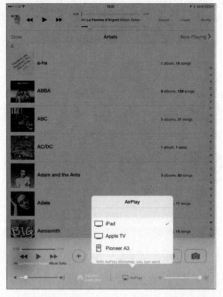

5 Set up Home Sharing To stream videos via AirPlay you need to turn on Home Sharing. Go to Settings, Videos, Home Sharing and enter your Apple ID and password.

6 Turn on AirPlay If you want music and video to play elsewhere, open Control Centre and tap AirPlay. You can now view the various AirPlay devices on your local network. Tap On to begin playback.

Change name You might be wondering how to change the name that appears in AirDrop. This is linked to your Apple ID, rather than your device's name. Tap Settings, iCloud, Account, Mail (under advanced) and change the Name field.

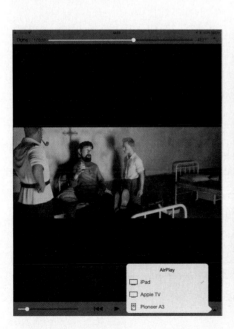

7 Streaming video You can also stream video to the Apple TV directly from the Videos app. Tap the AirPlay icon in the bottom left and choose Apple TV from the devices list.

8 Apple TV When the video is streaming your iPad will just display controls. You can use these to control the video playing through the Apple TV.

Checking how much storage each app is using

See which apps are using up the space on your phone

THE STORAGE CAPACITY OF THE iPAD HAS RISEN over the years, and it's now on par with a computer. Even so, filling up an iPad takes no time at all, especially with the video and music that you can so easily download from the iTunes Store. There is also now your iCloud account, which offers 5GB by default and needs to be managed.

KIT LIST:
- iPad
- iCloud account

Time required: 15 mins
Difficulty: Expert

It's not just photos and videos that fill up the storage space on your iPad, though. As apps get more complex and do more, they balloon in size.

It's entirely possible to fill up even a 64GB iPad just with apps. It's twice as easy to fill up a 32GB iPad, too. This would leave you no space for music, videos or any of the other fun stuff.

Thankfully, you can see which applications are taking up the most space. This is great if you are running low on storage and need to dump some apps you don't use. Remember that you can always re-download any of your apps. Deleting apps to make temporary space is easily done.

The ability to back up your iPad to iCloud is great for security, and this storage can also be managed on your iPad. See how much of your allowance you are using and buy more space if you need it.

Managing your precious storage space might seem a bit dull compared to all the other exciting things you could be doing on your iPad, but you can do it easily by following this simple tutorial.

▷

●●○○○ 3 ⏦　　　　　　　　　17:19　　　　　　　⬈ ✻ 99% ▮

Space left
You can quickly see how much space is left on your iPad in the Usage screen in the Settings app.

Se**ttings**

‹ General　　　　**Usage**

Airplane Mode

STORAGE
13.8 GB Available　　　　　　　42.8 GB Used

Wi-Fi　　　WiFidelity 5GHz

▶▶▶　Videos　　　　　　6.8 GB ›

Bluetooth　　　On

Photos & Camera　　5.9 GB ›

Mobile Data

XCOM　　　　　　3.2 GB ›

Personal Hotspot　　Off

Music　　　　　　2.6 GB ›

More details
To get more detail on an app and any further storage space it may be taking up simply tap on the app name.

arrier　　　　　3

KOTOR　　　　　2.2 GB ›

Comic Zeal　　　1.9 GB ›

Centre

Baldur's Gate　　1.8 GB ›

Control Centre

Xe　The Elements

Do Not Disturb

App size
Each app takes up a different amount of space, depending on what it does. You can see exactly how much space an app eats up right here.

Beethoven 9

Asphalt8

General

Show all Apps

Sounds

Wallpapers & Brightness

ICLOUD

Privacy

Total Storage　　　　　5.0 GB

Available　　　　　　1.7 GB

iCloud

Manage Storage　　　　›

Mail, Contacts, Calendars

Notes

BATTERY USAGE

Reminders

Battery Percentage

Messages

TIME SINCE LAST FULL CHARGE

FaceTime

Usage　　　　　　37 Minutes

1 See app size Go to Settings and tap on General, then Usage. Here you'll see a list of the top 10 space-eating apps. You'll also see the storage state of iCloud.

2 See all apps If you want to see the space taken up by all the apps on your iPad tap 'Show all Apps' and the list will expand.

3 **More app data** The actual size of an app isn't the only storage it consumes; some apps have documents and data that also take up space. Tap on an app to see how much it space needs.

4 **Delete an app** If you don't use an app and it's taking up space, or you just want to temporarily free up some space, tap on the app, then tap Delete App. This will get rid of it and all its data.

5 iCloud storage Your iCloud account includes 5GB of free space. You can review how much space you're using. Tap on Settings, then iCloud, Storage.

6 iCloud Backup You can back up your iPad to iCloud; simply turn on iCloud Backup. Tap on Settings, iCloud and turn on iCloud Backup.

Music app
Not all the apps and associated data can be removed; it's impossible to delete your Music app and songs, for example. This is good as the last thing you'd want to do is to accidentally delete all your music.

7 Backup in detail You can easily see if your backup is eating up your iCloud space by tapping on your iPad in Manage Storage. Trim the backup by turning off some items.

8 Space required If you need more storage space on the iCloud server you can always purchase up to 50GB a year from Apple. Tap on 'Change Storage Plan' to see how much it costs.

Pay just £2.99 an issue.

Get a 6-month subscription to PC Advisor for £19.99 or pick up 12 issues for just £35.88, saving 50%

Enjoy these benefits:

- ✓ ONLY £2.99 an issue (normal price £5.99)
- ✓ Save over 50% on the shop price
- ✓ Disc packed with the latest software and downloads
- ✓ PRIORITY delivery direct to your door each month

Every issue of PC Advisor is packed with the latest news, reviews and features, plus comprehensive, impartial buying advice and easy-to-understand tutorials to help you to get the most from your laptop, PC and tech gadgets. Each printed issue includes a free cover disc packed with the latest full-version Windows programs.

Weighing up the new iPads

Should the iPad have Touch ID finger scanning?
It's cool… but Jason Snell thinks we don't need it yet

I got my iPad Air this morning a little after 9AM. While I tried to gather some first impressions about Apple's new tablet at the office, I needed to retreat home to put it to the most important test: how does it work when I'm sitting on the sofa in my living room?

The iPad Air is dramatically lighter and noticeably smaller than its predecessor. My wife, who's currently using an iPad 3, was definitely impressed with the decreased weight.

I just finished up a FaceTime call with my mother, who got an iPad mini for Christmas last year. After a couple of months, she was still using her MacBook more than the iPad, and I was concerned that it was just a misbegotten purchase. But today she complained that the only reason she used her laptop anymore was to print, because her printer doesn't support AirPrint.

So even someone in their 70s who is as hesitant to embrace technology as my mother can fall under the spell

> Even someone who is as hesitant to embrace technology as my mother can fall under the spell of the iPad

of the iPad, given enough time.

I've been using the iPhone 5s since day one, and I admit that I've gotten used to Touch ID. It's great. I previously locked my iPhone with a four-digit passcode; now I use a more complex password, but almost never have to type it in. But here's the thing about the iPad: I've never, ever passcode-locked it. My iPad is generally in my house or in another secure location, and I just love the Smart Cover so much that I don't want to clutter up the experience by having to input a passcode.

It's hard, therefore, for me to regret a lack of Touch ID in a device that I've never locked. I understand Apple's choice to omit it from this generation of iPad – it just feels a bit less necessary than it does on the iPhone. Until then, I welcome our four-digit overlords.